May 1931

OLD ERRORS AND NEW LABELS

OLD ERRORS
AND NEW LABELS

By

FULTON J. SHEEN
Ph.D., D.D., LL.D.
Agrégé en Philosophie á l'Université de Louvain
The Catholic University of America

· THE CENTURY CO ·

NEW YORK

Nihil Obstat

ARTHUR J. SCANLAN, S.T.D.
Censor Librorum

Imprimatur

✠ PATRICK CARDINAL HAYES
Archbishop, New York

New York, March 2, 1931

First Printing

MARIÆ ILLIBATÆ QUAE VIRGO CAPUT SERPENTIS
ANTIQUI CONTRIVIT ERRORIS DISIECIT CALIGINEM
DEIPARA LUMEN VERITATIS AETERNÆ MUNDO EFFUDIT

There is only one reason for being critical, and that is to be constructive, just as the only reason for razing a house is to make one rise in its place. There is perhaps too much of the sceptic in the critic today, in the sense that his protests are rarely followed by reforms and his denunciations but seldom succeeded by enunciations. A need exists for a renewal of something implied in the word "appreciation," in the etymological sense, namely, an evaluation or a judging of things by their real worth. But the real worth implies a standard, and a standard of thinking cannot be the fashion, but what is true.

This book attempts just such an appreciation of contemporary ideas in the field of morals, religion, science, evolution, sociology, psychology and humanism in the light of that philosophical daylight called "common sense." If at times it criticizes certain views on the grounds of their unreasonableness, it does so

to prepare for a view which seems more reasonable. If at other times it shows that what is
wrong with a certain philosophical outlook is
that it emphasizes a part as against the whole,
it does so in order to suggest a view that is
more catholic in the sense of being the *whole*
truth.

There is no sympathy shown for those who
believe that everything that is modern is best,
nor with those who believe that everything
that is modern is bad. The book does attempt
to show, however, that what is often called
"modern" is only a new label for an old error,
and what is called "behind the times" is
really "beyond time" and outside of fashions,
like the truth of the multiplication table.

CONTENTS

ix

THE DECLINE OF CONTROVERSY

ONCE there were lost islands, but most of them have been found; once there were lost causes, but many of them have been retrieved; but there is one lost art that has not been definitely recovered, and without which no civilization can long survive, and that is the art of controversy. The hardest thing to find in the world to-day is an argument. Because so few are thinking, naturally there are found but few to argue. Prejudice there is in abundance and sentiment too, for these things are born of enthusiasms without the pain of labor. Thinking, on the contrary, is a difficult task; it is the hardest work a man can do—that is perhaps why so few indulge in it. Thought-saving devices have been invented that rival labor-saving devices in their ingenuity. Fine-sounding phrases like "Life is bigger than logic," or "Progress is the spirit of the age," go rattling by us like express-trains, carrying the burden of those who are too lazy to think for themselves.

Not even philosophers argue to-day; they only explain away. A book full of bad logic, advocating all manner of moral laxity, is not refuted by critics; it is merely called "bold, honest, and fearless." Even those periodicals which pride themselves upon their open-mindedness on all questions are far from practising the lost art of controversy. Their pages contain no controversies, but only presentations of points of view; these never rise to the level of abstract thought in which argument clashes with argument like steel with steel, but rather they content themselves with the personal reflections of one who has lost his faith, writing against the sanctity of marriage, and of another who has kept his faith, writing in favor of it. Both sides are shooting off fire-crackers, making all the noise of an intellectual warfare and creating the illusion of conflict, but it is only a sham battle in which there are no casualties; there are plenty of explosions, but never an exploded argument.

The causes underlying this decline in the art of controversy are twofold: religious and philosophical. Modern religion has enunciated one great and fundamental dogma that is at the basis of all the other dogmas, and that is, that religion must be freed from dogmas. Creeds and confessions of faith are no longer the fashion; religious leaders have agreed not to disagree and those beliefs for which some of our ancestors would have died they have melted into a spineless Humanism. Like other Pilates they have turned their backs on the uniqueness of truth and have opened their arms wide to all the moods and fancies the hour might dictate. The passing of creeds and dogmas means the passing of controversies. Creeds and dogmas are social; prejudices are private. Believers bump into one another at a thousand different angles, but bigots keep out of one another's way, because prejudice is anti-social. I can imagine an old-fashioned Calvinist who holds that the word "damn" has a tremendous dogmatic significance, coming to intellectual blows with an old-fashioned Methodist who holds that it is only a curse word; but I cannot imagine a controversy if both decide to damn damnation, like our Modernists who no longer believe in Hell.

The second cause, which is philosophical, bases itself on that peculiar American philosophy called "Pragmatism," the aim of which is to prove that all proofs are useless. Hegel, of Germany, rationalized error; James, of America, derationalized truth. As a result, there has sprung up a disturbing indifference to truth, and a tendency to regard the useful as the true, and the impractical as the false. The man who can make up his mind when proofs are presented to him is looked upon as a bigot, and the man who ignores proofs and the search for truth is looked upon as broadminded and tolerant.

Another evidence of this same disrespect for rational foundations is the general readiness of the modern mind to accept a statement because of the literary way in which it is couched, or because of the popularity of the one who says it, rather than for the reasons behind the statement. In this sense, it is unfortunate that some men who think poorly can write so well. Bergson has written a philosophy grounded on the assumption that the greater comes from the less, but he has so camouflaged that intellectual monstrosity with mellifluous French that he has been credited with being a great and original thinker. To some minds, of course, the startling will always appear to be the profound. It is easier to get the attention of the press when one says, as Ibsen did, that "two and two make five," than to be orthodox and say that two and two make four.

The Catholic Church perhaps more than the other forms of Christianity notices the decline in the art of controversy. Never before, perhaps, in the whole history of Christianity has she been so intellectually impoverished for want of good sound intellectual opposition as she is at the present time. To-day there are no foemen worthy of her steel. And if the Church today is not producing great chunks of thought, or what might be called *"thinkage,"* it is because she has not been challenged to do so. The best in everything comes from the throwing down of a gauntlet—even the best in thought.

The Church loves controversy, and loves it for two reasons; because intellectual conflict is informing, and because she is madly in love with rationalism. The great structure of the Catholic Church has been built up through controversy. It was the attacks of the Docetists and the Monophysites in the early centuries of the

Church that made her clear on the doctrine concerning the nature of Christ; it was the controversy with the Reformers that clarified her teaching on justification. And if to-day there are not nearly so many dogmas defined as in the early ages of the Church, it is because there is less controversy—and less thinking. One must think to be a heretic, even though it be wrong thinking.

Even though one did not accept the infallible authority of the Church, he would still have to admit that the Church in the course of centuries has had her finger on the pulse of the world, ever defining those dogmas which needed definition at the moment. In the light of this fact, it would be interesting to inquire if our boasted theory of intellectual progress is true. What was the Christian world thinking about in the early centuries? What doctrines had to be clarified when controversy was keen? In the early centuries, controversy centered on such lofty and delicate problems as the Trinity, the Incarnation, the union of Natures in the person of the Son of God. What was the last doctrine to be defined in 1870? It was the capability of man to use his brain and come to a knowledge of God. Now, if the world is progressing intellectually, should not the existence of God have been defined in the first century, and the nature of the Trinity have been defined in the nineteenth? In the order of mathematics this is like defining the complexities of logarithms in the year 30, and the simplification of the addition table in the year 1930. The fact is that there is now less intellectual opposition to the Church and more prejudice, which, being interpreted, means less thinking, even less bad thinking.

Not only does the Church love controversy because it helps her sharpen her wits; she loves it also for its own sake. The Church is accused of being the enemy of reason; as a matter of fact, she is the only one who believes in it. Using her reason in the Council of the Vatican, she officially went on record in favor of Rationalism, and declared, against the mock humility of the Agnostics and the sentimental faith of the Fideists, that human reason by its own power can know something besides the contents of test-tubes and retorts, and that working on mere sensible phenomena it can soar even to the "hid battlements of eternity," there to discover the Timeless beyond time and the Spaceless beyond space which is God, the Alpha and Omega of all things.

The Church asks her children to think hard and think clean. Then she asks them to do two things with their thoughts. First, she asks them to externalize them in the concrete world of economics, government, commerce, and education, and by this externalization of beautiful, clean thoughts to produce a beautiful and clean civilization. The quality of any civilization depends upon the nature of the thoughts its great minds bequeath to it. If the thoughts that are externalized in the press, in the senate chamber, on the public platform, are base, civilization itself will take on their base character with the same readiness with which a chameleon takes on the color of the object upon which it is placed. But if the thoughts that are vocalized and articulated are high and lofty, civilization will be filled, like a crucible, with the gold of the things worth while.

The Church asks her children not only to externalize their thoughts and thus produce culture, but also to internalize their thoughts and thus produce spirituality. The constant giving

10

would be dissipation unless new energy was supplied from within. In fact, before a thought can be bequeathed to the outside, it must have been born on the inside. But no thought is born without silence and contemplation. It is in the stillness and quiet of one's own intellectual pastures, wherein man meditates on the purpose of life and its goal, that real and true character is developed. A character is made by the kind of thoughts a man thinks when alone, and a civilization is made by the kind of thoughts a man speaks to his neighbor.

On the other hand, the Church discourages bad thinking, for a bad thought set loose is more dangerous than a wild man. Thinkers live; toilers die in a day. When society finds it is too late to electrocute a thought, it electrocutes the man. There was once a time when Christian society burned the thought in order to save society, and after all, something can be said in favor of this practice. To kill one bad thought may mean the salvation of ten thousand thinkers. The Roman emperors were alive to this fact; they killed the Christians not because they wanted their hearts, but because they wanted their heads, or better, their brains

—brains that were thinking out the death of Paganism.

It is to this task of thinking out the death of New Paganism that these chapters are written.

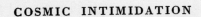

COSMIC INTIMIDATION

COSMIC INTIMIDATION

THE modern man is humble, not with that old humility which made a man doubt his power, but with the new humility that makes a man doubt his humanity. The old humility was grounded on truth: man is what he really is. The new humility is grounded on insignificance: man is only a speck in the cosmos.

This new attitude towards humility is not due to the advance of religion, but to the advance of astronomy. Telescopes and science have revealed to us the immensity of the universe. Those who are in a position to know inform us that the earth is but a tiny detail of that universe. The planet Jupiter, for example, has eleven times the diameter of the earth; fourteen hundred bodies the size of the earth could be packed into it and still have room to stretch. But that is not all: the stars are larger than Jupiter. It is the distance that belies their bulk. Recent measurement shows that the nearest stars are at almost exactly a million times

15

the distances of the nearest planets. Venus, for example, is twenty-six million miles distant from the earth, and the sun ninety-two million miles distant, while the nearest star, Proxima Centauri, is twenty-five million million miles away. Some of the stars, the Cepheids, are ten thousand times as luminous as the sun.

Because of the enormity of these distances, which cannot be understood in terms of miles, scientists have used a new measurement to make it intelligible, namely, the light-year. Light travels at the rate of 186,000 miles a second, and a light-year is therefore that number multiplied by 365 (days) by 24 (hours) by 60 (minutes) by 60 (seconds). In the language of a light-year, the nearest star is 4.27 light-years away from the earth. And yet this distance is trivial compared to the diameter of the galactic or starry system with its thirty thousand million stars, which is estimated to be two hundred and twenty thousand light-years. The radius of the entire universe is said to be two thousand million light-years; that is, it takes light traveling at the rate of 186,000 miles per second two thousand million years

16

to pass from one end of the universe to the other.

These figures are positively staggering. In some minds they have awakened a greater understanding of the Majesty and the Power of God, or a humility which recognizes that God is the Creator and Lord of all. In other minds they have developed an awe of the immensity of the cosmos or a humility which insists that man is nothing. In this latter class are certain really learned astronomers who prove to the world that a man may know his stars without knowing his logic.

This group has developed a philosophy of cosmic intimidation, by which they attempt to browbeat man into acknowledging his nothingness, because the cosmos is bigger than he. Such statements as the following "taken from life" are typical of the philosophy of cosmic intimidation. "The growth of modern science has brought about a comparable transformation of our attitude towards mankind. . . . Man tends to shrink in terms of the new cosmic outlook. Far from being the lord of all creation, existing from the beginning of things, he now appears to be but a temporary chemical episode on a most tiny planet." In the same tone, but in a manner as typical of the new humility, another writes: "The thing that appalls me is not the bigness of the universe, but the smallness of us. We are in all ways small—little in foresight, shriveled in spirit, minute in material content, microscopic in the vastness of measured space, evanescent in the sweep of time—inconsequential in every respect except perhaps in the chemical complexities of our mental reactions. Man is an animal among many, precariously situated on the crust of a planetary fragment, that obeys the gravitational impulses of one of the millions of dwarf stars that wander in the remote parts of one of many galactic systems."

Not content with reducing man to a "jelly-like semi-solid substance pigeonhole" in the cosmos, another writer believes that even the greatness of Our Divine Lord Himself is dwarfed in the immensity of the cosmos: "In our present cosmic perspective it would seem more reasonable to suppose that our particular solar system has not even been noted and catalogued in the astronomical star-chart of the cosmic Deity. That the cosmic God, if there be one, has ever taken special cognizance of the nebulous personality and uncertain teachings of a historically vague and inconspicuous religious teacher who lived in Palestine some two thousand years ago, represents a conception which can be entertained only by a person seriously circumscribed by ignorance or limited in intellectual power."

It takes a great deal of crust to call man a "crustal phenomenon," but it takes but little logic to show that such cosmic intimidation is built upon, first, an ignorance of the imagery of greatness, and secondly, two false assumptions: namely, that greatness is value, and that man was considered great in the old cosmology because he lived presumably in the center of the universe.

There is ponderous imagery in the modern scientific description of the universe, compared to which man is less than a speck in size. But this imagery of contrast between greatness and littleness is nothing new; the newness consists only in the subjects contrasted. The modern mind contrasts man with the universe and makes man nothing; the perennial mind contrasts God with the universe and makes the universe nothing. The first concludes to the pettiness of men from the greatness of the cosmos; the other to the pettiness of the cosmos from the majesty of God. It is much easier to dwarf a little thing like man than to dwarf a big thing like the universe. Modern imagery does the first; abiding revealed imagery does the latter, and for that reason is far more impressive. The imagery which tells me that there are thirty thousand million stars peopling the heavens as so many "tapers lit about the day's dead sanctities" is thrilling, but when my reason tells me these stars did not make themselves, nor did they come from nothing, the imagery evoked by the mention of One Who made them and Who "telleth the number of the stars and calleth them by name," makes the first image pass into insignificance. My imagination is taxed when the scientists describe the brightness of the sun as having $3^{27} \times 10^{27}$ candle-power, but it is overwhelmed when I am told that a "woman is clothed with the sun," and "the moon is under her feet." The imagery of the heavens as being two thousand million light-years in diameter is awesome when compared to the tiny earth, but trivial when compared to the imagery of the "hand that measured the heavens."

A normal mind looking at the vast expanse of the heavens is naturally and almost imperceptibly led to the conception of an Omnipotent Being Who threw them into space and endowed them with a law so that orb could pass by orb, and planet by planet, without ever a hitch or halt. It is an abnormal mind that begins immediately to think of pettiness when it sees power; it is not natural for a man who looks at a sky-scraper to think of the littleness of a flea, but rather of the greatness of the mind that conceived it. A great mural painting that covers the side of a corridor does not make a sane man think of a dwarf, but of an artist. When a modern mind stands amazed at the size of the cosmos and argues that even on this earth man is "far outdistanced by the cockroach," he is indulging in the same kind of fallacious reasoning that would make him conclude that L'Enfant, who designed the city of Washington, is only an infant, because the city of Washington is bigger and bulkier and therefore better than he is.

21

This brings us to the first false assumption underlying this type of anæmic thinking, namely, that greatness is to be measured by quantity rather than by quality.

The cult of magnitude is driving the modern mind mad; it has so obscured its mental vision as to blind it to other dimensions than those of length, breadth, and thickness. It is well to remember that the contained is generally worth far more than the container, even though the contained rattle around in the container like a diamond in a cracker-box. The really great things of the world are not always the immense things; great men are always little men in the sense that they are humble, as Cardinal Mercier was. They are so big they can always be seeming little, because it is only "seems." Sons of rich men can dress poorly, because they are really rich; they need not the panoply of the rich. Sons of poor men must dress richly to give the impression of wealth, because they are really poor. Greatness is not in size. Little things are much more impressive. Man never stumbles over a cosmos, though he does stumble over a rug. Concerning the confusion of greatness and value these few lines have been written: "If

22

God's lack of interest in us is because we are so little, then it must follow that He would take interest in us if we were enlarged. How large should we have to be before His interest began? If we were a hundred miles tall should we attract His attention? We may probably expect another negative. But if we towered up to a stature equivalent to the orbit of Neptune, we might possibly enter upon significance for Deity. And if we stood so high that our hair was singed by Betelgeuse—might we be admitted to the honor of audience with the Demiurge?

"Roaring nonsense? It is, indeed, but it is the roaring nonsense of very solemn and learned men who seem to shrink from thinking things out. They join together two incommensurable things—bulk, which has all the physical measurements, and meaning of value, which hasn't a single one. . . . But not only does the argument go thus far: it goes farther. It makes the higher of the two depend upon and be a function of the lower. It puts meaning or value as a secondary appendage to bulk. . . . Our learned friends, however, do not themselves adopt the valuation scheme which

23

they attribute to God. If they did, they would judge a small child to be worthless, a man of normal size barely acceptable, and a mountain of fatness a paragon of the day."

One moment a modern prophet tells us that man is great because he has evolved from matter: then in the next moment he tells us that he is nothing because matter is bigger than he is. They forget that though it is true that astronomy has displaced the earth as the center of the universe, it is equally true that biology has replaced man as its crowning center. Why magnify the science of astronomy at the expense of biology? They cannot have evolution of man from matter and the domination of matter over man, at one and the same time. Either evolution of man from matter, or the supremacy of matter over man, must be given up. The two theories are contradictory. It is nonsense to sing Swinburne's hymn, "Glory to man in the highest, for man is the master of all," and then the next moment let the "all" master the man and immerse him in the very matter from whence he has risen. Such theorists cannot eat their cake and have it.

Magnify and extol the heavens as much as

24

one pleases; multiply interstellar distances
unto a mathematical infinity; the fact still remains that man understands the heavens and
can interpret their movements in rational language. How could astronomers tell us about the
bulk of the heavens unless in some way they
got the bulk of the heavens into their heads—
a task that, incidentally, is less important than
the one of getting their heads into the heavens?
To get the cosmos inside of a head and still
have room on the inside of that head to look at
it, think about it, search out its laws, is to sit,
as it were, on the edge of still another great
mental cosmos and let one's feet dangle into
space, wishing all the while, like another Alex-
ander, that there were more worlds to conquer.

This whole problem of the dignity of man
was thought out years ago by Aristotle, who
called man a microcosm or a little universe, because he contained the cosmos within himself.
Man sums up the lower order of creation in a
double way: first, physically, and secondly,
mentally. Physically, he is made up of a combination of chemicals, vegetative processes,
and animal activities; he is like matter, because he exists; like plants, because he lives;

25

and like animals, because he feels. But he is above all these because he has his own peculiar perfection; namely, an intelligence, which enables him to know not only the phenomena of earth and the movements of the heavens, but the intelligibility of these phenomena in terms of causes and in particular, in terms of the First Cause, God.

The cockroach, which according to one's measurement has "remained unchanged for more than fifty million years," has seen many things evolve under his very eye. He has perhaps even seen bug-dynasties and flea-kingdoms rise and fall according to the Spenglerian formula, but the cockroach in all that fifty million years has never formulated even the simplest explanation of evolution that a man might formulate in an hour. It is that power to contain within his mind the infinitely great cosmos, and the infinitely little atom, and the infinite variety between the two, and to think of them all in the one thought—Order—that makes man the "beauty of the world and the paragon of animals." Science is but the reduction of multiplicity to the unity of thought, and just as there can never be science without a scientist, so neither can there be law and order in the cosmos unless it was made with law and order. The mind of man does not put law into the universe; it discovers it. If man discovers intelligibility there, some one must have put it there in making the cosmos intelligently. Thus the "very silence of the spheres" that frightened Pascal drove him on mentally until he found a Transcendent Source of Wisdom for that immanent order, which source is the Infinite God, to Whom be all honor and glory forever.

Those who refuse to unify the cosmos in terms of Pure Intelligence but content themselves with secondary causes may be likened to an all-wise mouse in a grand piano who laid the flattering unction to his soul that he had explained music by the play of hammers on the strings, the action of which he could see in his own narrow little world. "Scientists catch the tune but not the player."

The unification of the cosmos does not stop with man. Man has been met half-way on the upward progress by God, Who descended to earth and assumed his nature. In the circuits of the planets there are times when the heavens are under the earth, and in the ways of God

27

with men there was a time when Heaven was under the earth, and that was when Christ was born in the cave of Bethlehem. Just as in the world-order stars revolve about stars, planets and galactic systems around galactic systems, with a beautiful unity pervading all, so in the philosophical order, as all creation gravitates about man, either for his service, like the earth, or for his knowledge, like the cosmos, so does man gravitate towards creation's Creator. Man sums up the whole cosmos within himself. In assuming a human nature, then, Christ assumed in a certain sense the material world within His Immaculate Body, the whole spiritual world, intellectual and angelic, in His Pure Soul, and both of these touched the Divinity that was His by bonds of the Hypostatic Union—indissoluble bonds, stronger than love, stronger than life, stronger than time. Like a great and mighty pyramid the universe moves on to Unity under God. Man by his intellect masters the universe, subjugates it, rules over it, and possesses it within himself as knowledge; Christ, by assuming a human nature in the Unity of the Divine Person, brings all men to the Unity of His Law, His Peace, and His Life. He above all is fitted for the reconciliation of the finite in man to the Infinite in God, for He is both God and man, and to declare it to the world He died suspended between Heaven and earth, because He was the Pontiff, the *Pontifex*, the Bridge-Builder between the two. Such is the spiritual economy of a cosmic outlook that looks upon the cosmos not as a pluri-verse, but a uni-verse —things finding their unity in Christ, in accordance with that beautiful doctrine of Paul: "All are yours, you are Christ's and Christ is God's." What care we if Jupiter has more bulk than the earth? What matters it if Betelgeuse has more carbon than our tiny planet? Does that make dignity?

Not a star of all
The innumerable host of stars has heard
How He administered this terrestrial ball.
Our race have kept their Lord's entrusted Word.

Of His earth-visiting feat
None knows the secret—cherished, perilous;
The terrible, shame-faced, frightened, whispered, sweet
Heart-shattering secret of His way with us.

We know too much about matter to be materialists; we know too much about stars to think we are but star-dust. The galaxy of suns and starry worlds may boast of bulk and size and speed, but we too have our boast: Christ walked *our* earth.

AGNOSTICISM

AGNOSTICISM is an evil when it contends not only that an individual mind knows nothing, but also that no other mind knows anything. In this sense it is cowardly, because it runs away from the problems of life. Only about ten per cent of the people think for themselves. Columnists and head-line writers think for the greater per cent of the remainder. Those who are left are the agnostics, who think agnosticism is an answer to the riddle of life. Agnosticism is not an answer. It is not even a question.

There is, however, a sense in which agnosticism is desirable. In fact, a healthy agnosticism is the condition of increase of knowledge. A man may be agnostic in either one of two ways, either by doubting the value of things *below* him in dignity, or by doubting the value of things *above* him in dignity. Modern agnosticism doubts the things *above* man and hence ends in despair; Christian agnosticism doubts the value of things *below* man and hence ends in hope.

These statements admit of universal application. The universe may be compared to a temple made up of a vestibule, a sanctuary, and a Holy of Holies. Josephus in his "Antiquities" tells us that it was Jewish belief that the temple of Jerusalem with its three divisions was modeled on the plan upon which God built the universe, which too had its vestibule, its sanctuary, and its Holy of Holies.

The vestibule of creation or the material world is the world of the sun, moon, stars, plants, animals, and men—in a word, every sensible thing. The sanctuary of creation is the world of causes, of science, philosophy, and natural law. The Holy of Holies of creation is the world of mystery and revelation, such as the Trinity and the Incarnation. The same key that unlocks the vestibule of creation does not unlock the sanctuary of creation nor does the world of causes open the Holy of Holies. There are three keys for the temple. The first key that unlocks the world of matter is the five senses, by which we taste, see, touch, smell, and hear the material world and thus enter into communion with it. The second key that unlocks the world of causes, of purposes, is the key of reason, which enables us to penetrate the inner meaning and purpose of things. Finally, the key that unlocks the Holy of Holies of creation is the delicate key of faith.

Although there are three keys for this temple, we must not think that one part of it is opposed to the other. As a matter of fact, we go from the vestibule of creation to the sanctuary and from the sanctuary to the Holy of Holies by exactly the same kind of mental attitude, and that is the attitude of agnosticism. We may doubt one of two things, it was said above: either the value of things that are above man or the value of things that are below man. Modern skepticism doubts the value of things that are above man, such as Grace, the Divinity of Christ, the Trinity, and the perfection of man by a gift of God. But to doubt these things is to put an obstacle to progress and a bar to upward growth. This kind of agnosticism or even skepticism is really a species of septic poisoning. The other kind of doubt that doubts the value of things which are below—that is, the power of man to save himself, the possibility of this world's giving complete happiness, the capacity of science to satisfy the

35

human heart completely—is to make man look higher than this world and to open the path for further progress and perfection. To return to the point, I say that that process by which we pass from the vestibule to the sanctuary and from the sanctuary to the Holy of Holies of creation is by that latter kind of doubt or agnosticism.

There are then three sources of vision in this universe, each different in kind and yet each the perfection of the other—the eye, the reason, and faith. One unlocks the vestibule of creation or the material universe; the second unlocks the sanctuary of creation or the world of causes and finalities in the natural order; the third unlocks the Holy of Holies or the world of Incarnation and Grace. Observe now, how each reaches its perfection, namely, by a healthy agnosticism—an act of humility or a doubt. In other words, the ascent from the vestibule to the sanctuary, from the sanctuary to the Holy of Holies, is made thanks to a doubt. First of all, note that the eye is never constantly looking out on the material universe. It does not always enjoy the clear vision of the sunlight, even when the sun is shining. Every now

36

and then it must go into temporary darkness; every now and then it must have a doubt about its vision; every now and then it must be skeptical—and its skepticism is a wink. After the wink it opens itself and sees better; that is why light always seems doubly strong when we come out of a cave.

Reason too must follow the same law under the penalty of never coming to a clear vision and understanding of things. In moments of intense intellectual concentration we sometimes shut our eyes, bolt up the doors of sense-knowledge, in order that we may the more clearly bask in the light of reason. As the eye shuts out the light of day to enjoy it better the next moment, so the reason shuts out the light of mere experimental sense-knowledge in order that it may more clearly rejoice in the light of the mind. The *doubt* about the conclusiveness of material vision of the universe is the *wink* of reason, its momentary death to a lower life as a prelude to the riches of a higher one. The light of the intellect never shines so brightly as at the moment when it winks on the world of sense, but that doubt does not destroy the lower kind of vision, for when we have solved our intellectual problem in the sanctuary of our mind, we can open the doors of the senses once more, and for some very mysterious reason the eye sees things differently—"in a new light," as we often put it.

Now what holds true of the eye and mind, holds true of faith or the great world of the Incarnation continued by progressive filiation. How can we come to that full-orbed vision of faith? By no other means than by following what seems to be the most natural thing in the world—that restful act of winking—winking on reason, pulling down its shutters for a brief moment; in other words, doubting that reason can and does know all things knowable. This kind of wink is the most difficult of all; the very prospect of doing it makes us afraid that we may lose our reason, or go blind intellectually, but this is a groundless fear. The eye did not go blind because it winked on daylight, neither will the intellect go blind because it winks on science or reason. What will happen will be an improvement in the clarity of intellectual vision, an enlargement of its field and range, faith being to reason what a telescope is to the eye. It is during that first terrible moment of doubt about reason, that plaintive admission of healthy skepticism, "Help thou my unbelief," that God sends His gifts of Faith and Grace. Never once does this outlook on knowledge ask man to pluck out his eyes, or to extinguish the light of his reason. It asks him to use his reason, to use that first, to use it hard, to investigate Divine claims, but not to believe that reason can give the answer to all life's riddles. After a study, then a wink, then a doubt about the finality of reason, then a suspicion that there is a higher light, and then, aided by grace, the ascent to Faith. Once on those heights, then open the eyes, call up reason, verify, understand, and apply those mysteries of faith to the world of reason and sense. And so little by little new vistas of truth will open up, and what were even natural mysteries before will now glow with a new brilliance. Thus Faith is interpreted sometimes by Reason, and Reason holds up the hands of Faith until that last great temporary wink comes in the sleep of death, when we reopen our eyes to the unveiled vision of the Truth, which is God, the Light which is so bright that a celestial Jerusalem needs not a sun, for the sun is the Light of His Face.

This brings us back to our starting-point. The learned gentry of our modern world are unlearned because they never have a doubt. They try to make everything clear, and hence make everything mysterious. They forget that even nature has a mystery; that there is something in this great cosmos of ours which is just so terribly mysterious that we cannot "see" it, and that is the sun. It makes us wink whether we like it or not, and yet, in the light of that great natural mystery everything else in the world becomes clear. So too in higher realms, it is in the light of such a great supernatural mystery as the Incarnation that all things become clear, even the problem of evil.

ETHICS FOR THE UNETHICAL

THERE should be a vacation for certain over-worked words, and in particular the word "crisis." What "service" is to a Kiwanis booster, the word "crisis" is to moralists. This latter class have used it so often as to prove without doubt that Stevenson was right in saying that not by bread alone do men live but principally by catchwords. It is hardly possible to pick up a magazine to-day without reading an article by some self-styled ethicist on "The Crisis in Morals."

The repeated use of the word "crisis" in reference to morals is interesting, for it reveals a tendency on the part of many modern writers to blame the abstract when the concrete is really at fault. They speak, for example, of the problem of crime, rather than of the criminal; of the problem of poverty, rather than of the poor; and of the "crisis in morals," when really the crisis is amongst men who are not living morally. The crisis is not in ethics but in the unethical. The failure is not in the law, but in the law-breakers. The truth of this observation is borne out by the failure of such writers to distinguish between the problem of making men conform to standards and that of making standards conform to men. Instead of urging men to pass the test, they alter the test. Instead of inspiring them to hold to their ideals, they change the ideals. In accordance with this logic, they urge that morals be changed to suit those who cannot live morally, and that ethics be changed to please those who cannot live ethically. All this takes place in accordance with the democratic principle of certain philosophers, who are prepared to construct any kind of philosophy that man desires. If men want ghosts, the democratic philosophers, who know the will of the populace, will write a philosophy justifying ghosts; if the man in the street wants to follow the line of least moral resistance, philosophers will develop for him the justifying philosophy of "self-expression"; if the man of affairs has no time for the thoughts of eternity, then philosophers develop for him the philosophy of "space-time."

There are ultimately only two possible adjustments in life: one is to suit our lives to principles; the other is to suit principles to our lives. "If we do not live as we think, we soon begin to think as we live." The method of adjusting moral principles to the way men live is just such a perversion of the due order of things. Just suppose this logic were applied in the class-room. Boys and girls find it difficult to spell "knapsack" and "pneumonia," because the spelling of these words is not in the line of least phonetic resistance. Others, too, find it very hard to learn the multiplication table. Many a budding liberal mathematician cannot crush the urge to say that three times three equals six. Now here is a real "crisis" in spelling and mathematics, a kind of intellectual anarchy much akin to the moral anarchy described by our intelligentsia. How meet the "crisis"? One way to meet it is the way to meet any crisis, that is, by criticism; the other way to meet it is to write a new speller and a new mathematics entitled "A Preface to Spelling" or "Crisis in Mathematics." This is precisely what has taken place in the field of morals. Instead of making men conform to principles of morality, they change the principles. This kind

45

of philosophy would never have permitted the Prodigal Son to return to his father's house. It would have settled the "crisis" by finding a new and handsome name for the husks he was throwing to the swine, and called it "progress away from antiquated modes of morality."

All the books and articles on "the crisis in morality" touch on three points: the nature of morality, its origin, and its test. In discussing the general nature of morality, most authors reduce it to convention or taste. But before arriving at that conclusion they seem to sense the inadequacy of the very solution they propose, and one of them makes this rather excellent observation: "Social conventions change: the particular actions calculated to suit them change with them, as, e. g., if the rule of the road were changed in England we should drive on the right instead of the left. But the quality required for the right action does not change. It is just as important to drive carefully and considerately whatever the law of the road may be. The driver who says, 'First they say "left," then they say "right"; it is all a mess and I am free to be a road-hog' is indulging in a false argument."

So far, so good. But he immediately falls into the very logical pitfall he had asked others to avoid, for he makes two diametrically opposed moral principles akin to the convention of driving on the right or left side of the road. He writes: "So monogamy and polygamy are social conventions." In other words, for him there is no more difference between a moral system that permits a man to have one wife and a moral system that permits a man to have many wives, than there is between a traffic system that permits vehicles to drive on the right and another that permits vehicles to drive on the left. Now this is very poor logic. The difference between monogamy and polygamy is not the difference between the right side of the road and the left side of the road; it is a question of different roads, for monogamy is a one-road marriage, and polygamy is a boulevard. One could still be traveling in the proper direction whether he drove to the right as in America or to the left as in England. But he would not be doing so if he took an entirely different road, or a wrong road. Such is polygamy in relation to morality.

We agree with this philosopher in saying

47

that this conclusion is false: "First they say 'left,' then they say 'right'; it is all a mess and I am free to be a road-hog." Why, then, does he, who makes morality a convention, consent to make man a wife-hog, for such he does when he makes polygamy a matter of taste? If traffic laws and marriage laws are both conventions, why say the road-hog is wrong in one instance and not the wife-hog in the other instance? For the life of me, I cannot see why, if it is wrong to take up more than one half the road, it is not also wrong or more wrong to take up more than one better-half. Such authors' moral traffic needs regulation, and needs it badly.

Morality is evolutionary in its origin, according to this school of writers. This point is made in the following typical lines: "The point is that man, who has risen from the ape, has apparently done so by the help and guidance of this inward spirit which reject filth and denies it. It is not Victorian prudery, it is not Christian asceticism, it is not even the Hellenic tradition, which dislikes uncleanness, physical and moral; it is something that springs eternal in the nature of man."

There are enough errors in these two state-
48

ments to make a comedy of errors. Space will permit us to indicate only a few. If man "has risen from the ape," he has certainly done so in time, and not in eternity. How then can the author in the very next sentence speak of something "that springs eternal in the nature of man"? If there is something eternal in the nature of man, then man was always man, and did not come from the ape. If he did come from the ape, how could there be any eternal springs in his nature as man? Man, it is said, has apparently risen from the ape by the "inward spirit." Now, if man arose from the beast by this "inward spirit," then the "inward spirit" was already in man before he sprang from the ape, and he was man before he was an ape. The spring that enables jack-in-the-box to come from the box is already there, and we cannot say that the spring evolved from the box. Such philosophy puts the rabbit in the silk hat and pulls it out by evolution. Granting evolution, how account for the origin of morality from the ape? Imagine two apes fighting or prepared to fight in accordance with the evolutionary law of the survival of the fittest. Call one ape A, the other B. When locked in a death struggle, ape B is suddenly seized by an "inward spirit" of charity and a brotherly feeling for his fellow-ape. The dawning of reason tells him that ape A has a right to life, liberty, and the pursuit of happiness. And so ape B, in accordance with this first flash of morality, desists from the combat. Ape A wins the struggle; ape B goes to the grave with his "inward spirit." The first moral idea is lost to the world, and what happened to ape B would happen to every other ape in ape-land, for feelings of charity could never survive in an animal kingdom where might is right. The animal with the "higher urge to morality" would always succumb, and thus it would be impossible for such ideas ever to enter humanity through animality.

The great difficulty with evolutionary morals is to account for the "inward spirit" of morality. If it comes from the animal, then the animal should act like man; then man can always be expected to act like an ape because he came from one. If the "inward spirit" comes from above, that is, from God, then man can always be expected to act like God, because made to His own image and likeness. It seems very far-fetched for any moralist to become concerned

50

about a "crisis in morals" when his first principle is that man is only a glorified ape. The real crisis is not in morals but in logic—the logic that expects the amoral to produce the moral, and the monkey to produce the organ-grinder.

Finally, the new philosophy of morality offers æsthetics or "fastidiousness" as the test of morality. "As far as I can analyze my own feelings," one writes, "I should say that the motive which keeps me from a bad action is a feeling that as I contemplate it I do not like the look of it or the smell of it. I feel it to be ugly or foul or not decent—not the sort of thing with which I want to be associated. And, similarly, the thing that nerves me towards a good but difficult action is a feeling that it seems beautiful or fine, the sort of thing that I love as I look at it and would like to have for my own."

Here there is the false equation between feeling good and being good, and between feeling bad and being bad. What is wrong is not considered wrong but ugly, and what is right is not considered right but beautiful. The Scholastics were fond of saying that there is no disputing about tastes. The new morality would make taste the ground and foundation of morality. But the test of "fastidiousness" and "æsthetics" for morality leaves no basis for obligation. How apply it to debts? Will the bills at the end of the month be paid according to the principles of æsthetics or the principles of justice? Will only those statements printed on beautiful parchment receive our attention, while those printed on yellow foolscap are left unpaid? Will the thief of the new moral generation be exonerated because he looks like John Gilbert or be condemned because he looks like Ben Turpin? Will it be wrong for a future Volsteadian generation to drink rye because it is colorless and right to drink crème de menthe because of its beautiful emerald color?

Suppose this test of morality were applied to international conflicts. According to its principles, it would be wrong to go to war with Turkey because one does not "like the looks of it," but it would be right to go to war with Switzerland because its Alpine heights are "beautiful." By the same æsthetic test, adultery would be wrong if Mr. Smith's wife had lost her "school-girl complexion," but would be right if she had the "skin you love to touch." Murder would be wrong only for the man who, "analyzing his feelings," admits he does not like "the smell of it," but it would be right for the one who reduced it to a fine art. What the new morality resolves itself into is this: You are wrong if you do a thing you do not feel like doing; and you are right if you do a thing you feel like doing. Such a morality is based not only on "fastidiousness," but on "facetiousness." The standard of morality then becomes the individual feeling of what is beautiful, instead of the rational estimate of what is right.

The "smell of a thing" may be a good test for garlic, but is not a good test for morality. "The sort of a thing that I love as I look at it" may be a good test for a sunset, but there can be no end to moral confusion worse confounded if it is going to justify a violation of the ninth commandment, "Thou shalt not covet thy neighbor's wife"—with Protestants part of the tenth commandment. In a word, the fundamental difficulty with this system of morals is that it is impossible to be wrong—unless, perchance, one disagrees with its æsthetics.

A little less of æstheticism and a trifle more of asceticism would have made a happier morality. These moralists begin their search for a standard or test of morality with "human experience," or the "facts of life." In this they are right. Both Aristotle and St. Thomas Aquinas began their moral philosophy with both feet on the ground. First of all, they studied the way men lived and sought out their fundamental tendencies and aspirations. Thus far the French moralists of the Durkheim and Lévy-Bruhl school and the moralists under consideration are in agreement. Next, Aristotle and St. Thomas stated that these natural tendencies, such as the preservation of life, the propagation of life, and the self-expansion that results in private ownership, must be considered in relationship to the nature of man. But the nature of man is rational or intellectual. Here the modern moralists stop—they refuse to follow reason; "feelings" alone constitute the standard.

If the nature of a man is rational, then these tendencies must be judged rationally. But to judge anything rationally is to judge it in relation to the end or purpose for which it was

54

created. A pen is to be judged by its capacity for writing, but that is why it was made; an eye is to be judged by its powers of vision, for that is the reason of its being. Man was made for a perfect fruition of his desire and striving for Life, Truth, and Love, which is God. Man, therefore, is to be judged in relation to this end, that is, in his submission to or rebellion against it. In other words, man has duties to God and God is entitled to them, for the same reason that every author is entitled to royalties on his books, because they are his creation. This fulfilment of our duties to God, this obedience to His will, which is synonymous with the perfect development of our whole nature, is the ground and basis of morality. Morality, then, is order in relation to an end. And that all things might tend to their own proper destiny, Almighty God has placed in the various hierarchies of creation an immanent law to guide them. The laws of nature, such as gravitation, chemical affinity, and the like direct the chemicals to the fulfilment of their natures. The laws of life, such as metabolism, guide plants to the perfection of their destiny. Instincts guide animals, and reason directs man. The practical reason of man that enables him to fit particular cases under the general principles touching his final destiny is conscience.

So, first, morality means a conscious relation between the nature of man and the goal of his being; and secondly, it entails an immanent principle of guidance in the work, which is conscience. The immanent law in creation below man is unconscious and necessary. Hence, an acorn works out its destiny naturally: it grows to be an oak. Man, however, is free to stunt his growth, and to choose another end than the efflorescence of his faculties in union with Perfect Love. If man chooses, he need not grow up to be an oak; he can remain a poor sapling or just a "poor sap." And that is what this new school of morality would make of each of us.

THE WAX NOSE OF SCIENTIFIC AUTHORITY

THE WAX NOSE OF SCIENTIFIC
AUTHORITY

EVERY now and then pronouncements are made concerning the alleged conflict of science and religion and among these the statement of a scientist about religion is generally given a value which it really does not possess. Among the most important utterances of scientists in our day on this subject are those of Sir Arthur Eddington and Sir James Jeans.

Speaking of the omniscient science of the last century, Sir Arthur Eddington said: "Materialism and determinism; those household gods of nineteenth century science, which believed that the world could be explained in mechanical or biological conceptions as a well-run machine, each cog of which moved in relation to other cogs, must be discarded by modern science." Striking the same key, Sir James Jeans observes: "No scientist who has lived through the last thirty years is likely to be too dogmatic, either as to the future course of the stream or as to the direction in which reality lies: He knows from his own experience how the river not only forever broadens, but also repeatedly winds, and after many disappointments he has given up thinking at every turn that he is at last in the presence of the murmurs and scents of the Infinite Sea . . . so that our main contention can hardly be that the science of today has a pronouncement to make, perhaps it ought rather to be that science should leave off making pronouncements: The river of knowledge has too often turned back on itself."

Not only do these two distinguished men of science repudiate the old notion that science has already spoken the last and unchanging word about reality, but they also suggest that science leaves room for, and almost demands, God. Sir Arthur writes in this connection: "The spiritual element in our experience is the creative element and if we remove it, as we are trying to do in Physics on the ground that it always creates an illusion, we must reach what was in the beginning [chaos]. . . . It means a great deal to me to conceive of God as Him through Whom comes power and guidance." Sir James Jeans is even more emphatic. After having explained that the whole material world is resolved to waves and that these waves are of two kinds—bottled-up waves that we call matter, and unbottled waves that we call radiation or light—he adds: "These concepts reduce the whole universe to a world of light, potential or existent, so that the whole story of its creation can be told with perfect accuracy and completeness in the six words 'God said: Let there be light'." "This Creator," he believes, "is not so much an engineer as a mathematician, that is to say, one who lives in the realm of pure thought and, what is equally important, He is outside of space and time." "Modern scientific theory," he says, "compels us to think of the Creator as working outside time and space, which are part of his Creation, just as the artist is outside his canvas. *Non in tempore sed cum tum tempore finxit Deus mundum*.'"

Fundamentalists, who have no supreme court behind their Book and hence hold rather unscientific notions concerning the universe, have held these statements as dealing a death-blow to the oft-repeated assertion that there is conflict between religion and science. There has been a tendency, perhaps, for every one who is interested in eternal verities to look upon these two pronouncements as final and really authoritative, and to argue that there is no conflict between religion and science because Sir James and Sir Arthur, who are both scientists, tell us there is no such conflict. There is a great danger that the words of these two scientists will be exaggerated out of due importance, and it is for that reason that we wish to make two reflections: one to indicate a caution, and the other to point a moral.

It is well to remember that authorities in the field of science are really opinions, and that such authorities have a wax nose and can be led anywhere one chooses. While it is quite true that Sir James and Sir Arthur do deny that there is a conflict, there are dozens of others who assert emphatically that there is a conflict. It behooves us, therefore, not to think that the last and final pronouncement has been made on this subject, nor to put too much credence in or to place too much value on them, and for these two reasons:

First, the methods of science and religion differ, and hence because a man becomes a specialist in one method, it does not follow that he is also a specialist in the other. A scientist works on material things through the help of mathematical symbols, but a philosopher who treats of religion works on spirit, which by its very nature is outside the scope of empirical science. The scientist handles concrete facts like bones, rays of light, chemicals, and his interest goes little further than the behavior of these things. When he wishes to test a conclusion that he has reached concerning the behavior of facts, he goes back to the facts themselves and repeats his experiment from every possible angle. The philosopher, on the contrary, is concerned not with the behavior of facts, but with certain abstractions drawn from facts, such as the existence of truth, beauty, and goodness. His concern is not to discover the behavior of these things, but rather to seek out their ultimate origin. When finally he has reached a conclusion concerning the origin of these things, which is God, he does not test it by going back to the facts themselves as does the empirical scientist, but rather tests it in the light of certain first principles, like the principle of contradiction, the principle of causality, or the principle of finality. The scientist, in other words, is interested in secondary causes, the philosopher in primary causes. The scientist is concerned with the tune that is being played; the philosopher is interested in the player. The very moment that a scientist ceases to concern himself with *how* things happen and to interest himself in the question *why* they happen, he ceases to be a scientist and automatically becomes a philosopher.

Science, therefore, by its very nature, since it deals with facts, tested by facts, can never give us any knowledge about the ultimate with which religion is concerned. Thus, when Professor Jeans and Professor Eddington declare themselves in favor of a mind behind the universe, they are not speaking as scientists but as philosophers, and are using different methods to make their great discovery than they used to make their discovery about radiation, and hence their conclusions for the existence of God are only worth the reasons they give for it.

A different question now presents itself: Is the man of science as adept in the methods of philosophy as he is in the methods of experimentation? There is hardly any one vain enough to say that he is. In fact, the chances are that he will be less skilful in the method of philosophy, for the constant handling of the concrete dulls his capacity for handling the abstract. Philosophy is a form of spirituality, and its first condition is abstraction from matter. A word of caution, then, is necessary when a statement is made by a scientist turned philosopher, just as a word of caution is necessary when a statement is made by a philosopher turned scientist, or an automobile manufacturer turned historian, or an oil man turned authority on church unity. This does not mean to imply that all the wrong is on the side of the scientists. Very often philosophers and theologians commit the same fallacy by passing premature judgments in the conclusions of science. A philosopher who attacks Einstein because he knows nothing about the mathematical aspect of relativity would be just as absurd as Einstein, who apparently knows no theology, is when he attacks religion and contends that its basis is fear. That same prudence which makes us accept soberly the testimony of scientists in favor of God, though it happens to be the right testimony, is the same that makes us refuse to believe that because Einstein knows a great deal about the relativity of space and time, he therefore knows a great deal about the Spaceless beyond space and the Timeless beyond time. Since the methods of science and religion differ, competency in one field does not mean competency in the other. Not only that. Since the methods of the two differ, there will be a great difference in the certitude attained by the method of science and the certitude attained by the method of philosophy (we are still continuing to speak of natural religion). Science arrives at only probable conclusions, says Jeans and others. We believe this, but not only because Jeans says so.

Our reason for believing that science is not final or conclusive is not because any particular scientist tells us so, but rather because of the nature of science itself. The argument that we are about to give is taken from the great philosopher of the Middle Ages, St. Thomas Aquinas, who in commenting on the works of Aristotle reasoned as follows: Science deals not with individuals but with natures that are common to individuals. For example, the psychologist studies not John Jones as John Jones, but John Jones inasmuch as he is a man and participates

66

in the nature of man. Man is therefore the *experimentable*. John Jones and John Smith and any other individual that the psychologist studies constitute the *experimented*.

Now there is a great difference between the *experimentable* and the *experimented*. The *experimentable* is infinite because there is no limit to the number of individuals who may participate in the nature of man. The *experimented*, on the contrary, is finite, because the psychologist or the scientist cannot experiment on every man in the universe. There is, therefore, going to be a tremendous disproportion between the experimentable and the experimented—between the experiments he may perform and those he actually does perform—and hence the scientist must content himself with a probable conclusion.

The conclusions of philosophy, when it touches natural religion, are not tarred with the same stick. Philosophy reasons from universal and necessary propositions, and hence reaches necessary and certain conclusions. It is not my point to prove this assertion, although it is an assertion that can readily be proved. Rather, the point is to emphasize that the conclusions of science are problematic, and that is the reason for frequent change of scientific theories, whereas the proof of the existence of God and the necessity of religion is not problematic, but certain, and that is the reason for unvarying belief in it on the part of humanity.

In brief, science is concerned only with secondary causes, and philosophy with primary ones. It would therefore be very unbecoming for any one to say that because science is discovering laws, such as gravitation, therefore God is no longer necessary. Almighty God could very well say: "Because nature obeys Me, do you believe it renders Me useless, and that the laws which I have made suffice, without Me, to explain My work?" A law implies a lawmaker, and a mathematical universe implies a mind, and an organic universe implies life somewhere in its source. Scientific laws are indeed important, but it is much more important to know God.

The whole contrast between the Middle Ages, which sought the primary cause, and the modern age, which seeks the secondary cause, can be exemplified by art. In the Middle Ages no sculptor ever chiseled his name on a statue.

The reason was that he was working for God, and it was God Who gave him the power to cut, and Who gave him the mind to be an artist, and when he left his work anonymous, God, the First Cause, received the credit. In our own day, the sculptor chisels his name on his marble because he is working for man, and has forgotten the First Cause and the Cause of all causes, which is God.

The second reason for caution in the acceptance of authority concerning the alleged conflict of religion and science, is that that which makes a man religious is not the same thing as that which makes a man scientific. I do not mean to say that religion and science are contraries, but merely that a man is religious by virtue of something else than that by which he is scientific. A man who makes a good church janitor does not necessarily make a good Christian, because that which makes him a good janitor is not the same thing as that which makes him a good Christian. A few years ago, one of the large New York city churches missed money from its poor-boxes. Detectives hidden in the church during the night saw the janitor come before the altar, make a genuflexion, and then rob the poor-boxes—and all the while he was a good janitor. Keeping a soul clean is a different matter than keeping a church clean. There is, therefore, an element in soul cleanness that is not in church cleanliness.

So too in the problem of religion and science —there is something in religion that is not in science. There is knowledge in both religion and science, but the will plays a part in religion that it does not play in science, and it is his will that makes a man morally courageous, and not his knowledge. Theoretically, there should be a balance between knowledge and love, which is seated in the will—as there is in the Trinity, where the Son and Holy Spirit are equal—but practically, this is not true. There is many a professor of theology who knows a great deal about theology but who dies a Doctor of Divinity and not a saint, and there is many a man who knows but little of theology and less of science but who dies full of the love of God.

Profound science, therefore, does not mean profound religion, any more than profound religion means profound science. Some scientists know science, but teach immorality; others know science, but teach morality. This proves

70

there is something else besides scientific knowledge in morality and religion, and that something else is the will to let correct knowledge or truth determine our lives, instead of letting our lives determine truth. The testimony of scientists in favor of religion is satisfying indeed, but it must not be exaggerated, for, I repeat, that which makes a man a saint is not necessarily the same as that which makes him a savant.

In addition to this caution, it perhaps might be well to point a moral concerning the testimony of these two really distinguished men of science. When Sir Arthur Eddington delivered his statement a New York newspaper head-lined: "Day of Materialism Over," and devoted over two columns to his testimony. Another gave a column and a half of its valuable space and head-lined: "Stick to Religion. It's Nearer Truth Than Science." Why is it that these two important newspapers both gave so much space to the statement that materialism is dead? It can only be because for the journalistic world that statement constitutes news, but really it was no news at all, for there is hardly any one who has been conversant with scientific progress during the last twenty or thirty years who has ever believed otherwise.

Those who have had their fingers on scientific progress know very well that the materialistic and deterministic scientific outlook of the nineteenth century is now quite a thing of the past. Dingler in Germany; Boutroux, Poincaré, and Duhem in France; Keynes, Campbell, and Dampier-Whetham in England; and Lewis and Whitehead in America—all these have broken entirely with the nineteenth-century tradition. There is, therefore, really no news value in the head-line that materialism is dead. Why, then, was so much space given to it? The answer, I believe, is to be found in a mood typical of our own day, namely, the mood of Modernism. It has been our contention that Modernism is nothing new, but only a new complexion for the old face of error, or a new label for an old error, and hence the only reason a man is a Modernist is because he does not know what is ancient. Here is the explanation for the head-line. It was quite new to the Modernist, who does not know what is ancient, but it was not new to us who have always known

72

that the day of materialism was over—in fact, we knew that back in our childhood days when we learned that man has an immortal soul and that God is Pure Spirit.

THE THEISM OF ATHEISM

No self-respecting periodical that boasts of its twentieth-century outlook is complete without an article once every few months on the subject: "Do we need a new God?" Just as there are those who believe we should change morality to suit our amorality, so there are those who believe we should change God to suit our godlessness.

Attitudes concerning the new God have been divided between the camp of the Fundamentalists and that of the Modernists, both of which groups believe that there is no other religious group in the world. It is worth remarking at the outset that there really is another in the world, which numbers over three hundred million adherents, and which prides itself on being neither Fundamentalist nor Modernist—and that is the Catholic Church. It is not Fundamentalist, because more fundamental than Fundamentalism; it is not Modernist, because more modern than Modernism.

Fundamentalism assumes that the Bible is fundamental. Catholicism retorts, as is pointed out elsewhere in these pages, that the Bible is not a book but a collection of books, and hence the question more fundamental than Fundamentalism is: Who gathered the books together, and declared that they would constitute a Bible, and be regarded as the revealed Word of God? To answer this question is to get to a body beyond a book, namely, a Church with a spirit; for Pentecost was not the descent of books on the heads of the Apostles but the descent of tongues. From that day on it was to be a tongue and a voice, and not a book, that would be fundamental in religion.

The Church is not only more fundamental than Fundamentalism, but she is also more modern than Modernism, because she has a memory that dates back over twenty centuries; and therefore she knows that what the world calls modern is really very ancient—that is, its modernity is only a new label for an old error. Modernism has an appeal only to minds who do not know what is ancient, or perhaps antiquated. The Church is like an old schoolmaster who has been teaching generations and genera-

78

tions of pupils. She has seen each new generation make the same mistakes, fall into the same errors, cultivate the same poses, each believing it has hit upon something new. But she, with her memory, which is tradition, knows that they are making the same mistakes all over again, for in the wisdom born of the centuries she knows very well that what one generation calls modern the next generation will call unmodern. She knows also that Modernism is no more logical than a sect called "Three O'Clockism," which would adapt our gods and our morals to our moods at three o'clock. The Church knows too that to marry the present age and its spirit is to become a widow in the next. Having constantly refused to espouse the passing, she has never become a widow, but ever remains a mother to guide her children and to keep them not modern but ultra-modern, not behind the times but behind the scenes, in order that from that vantage-point they may see the curtain ring down on each passing modern fad and fancy.

The arguments for the "new God" are generally twofold: first, the times demand it, and secondly, science requires it. Two false assumptions underlie these arguments, and the first is the confusion between a *fact* and an *idea*. There is a world of difference between "God" and "the idea of God." If I see a canary and call it a giraffe, I must revise my idea to suit the fact, the canary remaining a canary all the while. But if I am an architect, I may revise a house to suit my idea of the house or of an ideal house. In the first case, I change the idea to fit the fact; in the second, I change the fact to suit the idea. The two are not the same; in fact, the one condition that makes it possible for me to change the fact to suit my idea is that I be the creator, or cause of the fact.

Applying this to God, the demand for a new God must mean either one of two things: either we must change the idea of God to suit God, or else we must change God to suit our new idea of God. In the first case, to change the idea to suit God is meaningless if God is unchanging. If He is unchanging, it is nonsense to say that God was one thing in the days of Israel and is another in the days of science. This is just like saying that two apples plus two apples made four apples in the days of Isaias, but do not in the days of Einstein.

In the second case, if we must change God to suit our idea, then we create God. Now this God we create is greater or less than we are. If He is greater than we are, then the greater comes from the less; if He is less than we are, then it is folly to speak of Him as a God.

As for the necessity of coining new names for God, it is incomprehensible to a thinking mind that philosophy and civilization can be enriched by ceasing to think of God as Life, Truth, Beauty, and Love, and beginning to think of Him as a blind and whirling space-time configuration dancing dizzily in an Einstein universe, plunging forward along a path of which He is ignorant, toward a goal of which He knows nothing whatever. It is much easier to worship the God who made life than the God who is a "space-time epochal occasion."

Another assumption that vitiates the logic for the new God is that it hypostatizes science. "Modern science repudiates God," it is said. Now just what is "science"? Renouvier used to say: "I should very much like to meet that person every one is talking about—that person Science." They talk of science as if it were just as real as themselves; they draw portraits of *its*

81

conclusions, sketches of *its* godlessness, they state demands of *its* new visions, when all the while there is no *it*—there is only a *their* and *theirs*—and that means *scientists*, which is as different a thing from science as "John" is different from "humanity."

It is a rather curious fact that the same bad logic that infected the Reformation of revealed religion in the sixteenth century infects the Reformation of natural religion in the twentieth century. The first instance of illogical reasoning is concerned with the necessity of a reformation and the second with its method.

In the sixteenth century a reformation was needed. Now there were two reforms possible: one was to reform faith, the other was to reform discipline. The faith was solid; it was the Faith of Christ. The discipline, however, was weak, for it was the discipline of worldliness. The reformers, who sometimes reform the wrong thing, reformed faith instead of discipline, and brought revealed religion to the present state of "confusion worse confounded."

In the twentieth century a reformation in philosophy is needed. Two reforms are possible: one is to reform the principles of philosophy, the other is to reform its discipline, or make men think correctly. The Modernist believes we should reform the principles, eliminate God from religion as we might eliminate animals from zoölogy or life from biology or marble from sculpture. We contend that the principles of reason are sound and the heritage of common sense. What is needed is a little mental discipline, sound logic, correct thinking, and a cessation of anemic reasoning. In the first year of elementary-school life the little students make all manner of multiplication tables, some saying that two times two make six, and others that four times four make forty. The teacher, in the face of this mental riot, does not permit herself such broad-mindedness as to believe that the multiplication table should be reformed; she reforms the mental discipline of the children and sets them on the right path. Why should not philosophers do likewise? Perhaps the solicitation to pamper the way men live is too strong for them, for much of the business of philosophy at the present time seems to be to give high-sounding names to cover the sins of men. The clay is now molding the potter and the marble carving out the sculptor.

Not only as regards the necessity of a reformation, but even as regards the method, is there a similarity between the sixteenth century and the twentieth century. Then the various sects pulled the miter and the head off pontifical man, and the spirit of unity went out from the body. A new rule of faith was sought for and found in the Bible. The question then arose: Who gathered the books together? These questions never were answered. A timid, thin-skinned solution was found by substantizing the books and calling them a Book—to make men forget the problem of its origin.

Now in the twentieth century an identical process is taking place. The soul has gone out from psychology as the spirit went out from theology. The soul is the principle that unifies—the principle that grouped together the various findings of scientists and called it "science." The problem that arises in these days of soulless philosophy is: Who gathered the findings of scientists together and made them a unity and made it possible to call them "science"? A new solution, a false one, has been found by substantivizing the scientists and calling them "science." But this is no real inward unity, only an incoherent, contradictory mass of evidence with no common bond other than a name. The soul that grasped these conclusions in a synthesis of truth has given way to a kind of scientific pantheism in which science may stand for anything from the crudities of Draper and White to the niceties of Einstein. Take the spirit of truth from the Bible and there is nothing to unify the books; take the soul of truth from science and there is nothing to unify the scientists. In neither case is one down to fundamentals, and it remains for certain modern philosophers who are Fundamentalists in science, to explain the unity of science without a soul, as it remains for Fundamentalists in religion to explain the Bible without a spirit.

The philosophical appeal for a new God is at bottom nothing but a form of atheism. There are two ways of being an atheist: one is to say, "There is no God"; the other is to say, "We need a new idea of God and that God is Space-Time, or the ideal tendency in things." One of the things I could never understand about this second kind of atheism, is how certain minds could admit that the universe is God and still deny that a man might be God—I mean Christ. Another thing equally difficult to understand is how certain humanitarians could say that God is the society of the millions and millions of persons living to-day, and yet deny that there could be three persons in God—I mean the Trinity.

The denial of God is really not a doctrine; it is a cry of wrath. If atheism means a denial that this universe demands a cause of its being, whatever it be, there are probably few atheists, if any. One of the most famous atheists of modern times, M. Le Dantec, says that "many call themselves atheists without knowing what they mean." Some call themselves atheists when their atheism does not mean the denial of a cause, but only the ignoring of it. With others, atheism is identified with the law of the universe—as if there could be a law without a lawmaker. But it is extremely doubtful if there are any who deny God in the sense that their denial would imply that the universe caused itself. Such a position is rationally impossible, for if the universe caused itself, it would need to have preëxisted itself, in order to bring itself into being—which is nonsense.

One may therefore justly speak of the theism of atheism, for the very denial of God asserts in some way His existence. Suppose I began circulating the country with pamphlets fighting the belief in fairies, and ghosts, and goblins, and cows that jumped over moons; suppose I wrote books against three-legged centaurs, and against ghosts that floated like Ivory Soap; suppose I used the radio to warn the American public against the Sandman who sprinkles sand in the eyes of children after nine o'clock. What would be the reaction of the general public? They would probably lock me up as a madman and a public nuisance—and rightly so, because I would have proved beyond doubt that I was insane, for what is insanity but a belief in the figments of the imagination?

Now suppose that God, as the atheists hold, is no more real than these centaurs and fairies; suppose God belongs to that same queer and weird group of fancies as the three-legged ghost. Now I ask, why is it that society would consider me insane if I spent myself and was spent in the campaign against cows that jumped over the moon, and yet would not consider the atheist insane, because he carries on a campaign to prove that God belongs to that same class of fancies and imaginings?

The reason is obvious. The atheist is not mad; he is not insane. What I would be fighting against would be a figment of my imagination, but what the atheist is fighting against is a reality—something as real as the thrust of a sword or an embrace. A man is mad who imagines a fancy to be real, but the atheist is not fighting against a fancy that he imagines to be real, but a reality that he takes to be a fancy. In other words, what saves the atheist from the stigma of insanity is the fact that he is fighting the Reality by which all things else are real. Foch was not insane when he took gray uniforms at Rheims to be the uniforms of an enemy; it is the objectivity of the enemy that makes the attack sane and sound, and it is the objectivity of the enemy of atheism that saves atheists from being mad, though it does not save them from being sad. That is why one may speak of the theism of atheism.

Certain things are so fundamental that to

deny their existence is to assert them. For example, if I deny that I exist, I imply my own existence, for I have to exist before I can deny my existence. The denial implies an affirmation, and in a still more general way, the denial of the Principle of all existence implies the existence of that Principle. If there were no wines nor liquors we would never have prohibition. The very fact that there is a league against saloons—the Anti-Saloon League—implies the failure of prohibition and the existence of saloons, or at least of speak-easies. If there were never any cigarettes, there would never be any anti-cigarette laws, and if there is no God, how can there be atheism? Does not atheism imply something to "atheate"?

The only reason in the world for loving life and love and truth is because they come from God, and if they do not come from God then there is no good reason for loving them. The very same reasoning process that makes other things intelligible is that which makes God intelligible, Who is the source of abiding values and realities. Our great minds of to-day turn their telescopes on Mars and see there something that faintly resembles canals. They then argue: there are canals on Mars, but only an intelligent being can make a canal; therefore Mars must be inhabited by men. Now, I cannot understand for the life of me why if it is logical to conclude to a canal-builder from the sight of a canal, it is not logical to conclude to a universe-builder from the sight of the universe. Other minds there are who turn over the blistering sand of the Egyptian desert, discover a few tombs and relics, and then from that paltry evidence reconstruct the nature of the civilization of those days. Now if this is logical—and it is logical—why should not those same minds infer something of the Justice, the Goodness, and the Beauty of God from the vestiges of those things found here in this universe? If, too, there are minds in the world who believe that the universe is guided by purpose, why should they not admit God, for how can there be purpose without a mind, and how can there be mind unless it be a Person?

No! A godless universe cannot exist, for it cannot bear the sorrow of not knowing its Author and its Cause; nor can a godless humanity exist, for it cannot bear the burden of its own heart. That is why I always feel sorry for the atheist: he never can say "Good-by" (God be with you) to his friends.

A PLEA FOR INTOLERANCE

A PLEA FOR INTOLERANCE

AMERICA, it is said, is suffering from intolerance. It is not. It is suffering from tolerance: tolerance of right and wrong, truth and error, virtue and evil, Christ and chaos. Our country is not nearly so much overrun with the bigoted as it is overrun with the broad-minded. The man who can make up his mind in an orderly way, as a man might make up his bed, is called a bigot; but a man who cannot make up his mind, any more than he can make up for lost time, is called tolerant and broad-minded.

A bigoted man is one who refuses to accept a reason for anything; a broad-minded man is one who will accept anything for a reason— providing it is not a good reason. It is true that there is a demand for precision, exactness, and definiteness, but it is only for precision in scientific measurement, not in logic.

The breakdown that has produced this unnatural broad-mindedness is mental, not moral. The evidence for this statement is threefold:

the tendency to settle issues not by arguments but by words, the unqualified willingness to accept the authority of any one on the subject of religion, and, lastly, the love of novelty.

Voltaire boasted that if he could find but ten wicked words a day he could crush the "infamy" of Christianity. He found the ten words daily, and even a daily dozen, but he never found an argument, and so the words went the way of all words and the thing, Christianity, survived. To-day, no one advances even a poor argument to prove that there is no God, but they are legion who think they have sealed up the heavens when they have used the word "anthropomorphism." This word is just a sample of that whole catalogue of names which serve as the excuse for those who are too lazy to think. One moment's reflection would tell them that one can no more get rid of God by calling Him "anthropomorphic" than he can get rid of a sore throat by calling it "streptococci." As regards the use of the term "anthropomorphism," I cannot see that its use in theology is less justified than the use in physics of the term "organism," which the new physicists are so fond of employing. Certain words like "reactionary" or "medieval" are tagged on the Catholic Church and used with that same disrespect with which a man might sneer at a lady's age. Mothers do not cease to be mothers because their sons grow up, and the Mother Church of the Christian world, which began not in Boston but in Jerusalem, is not to be dispossessed of her glorious title simply because her sons leave home. Some day they may be glad to return and their return will be the truest "home-coming" the world has ever seen.

Not only does the substitution of words for argument betray the existence of this false tolerance, but also the readiness on the part of many minds to accept as an authority in any field an individual who becomes a famous authority in one particular field. The assumption behind journalistic religion is that because a man is clever in inventing automobiles he is thereby clever in treating the relationship between Buddhism and Christianity; that a professor who is an authority on the mathematical interpretation of atomic phenomena is thereby an authority on the interpretation of marriage; and that a man who knows something about illumination can throw light on the subject of

97

immortality, or perhaps even put out the lights on immortality. There is a limit to the transfer of training, and no man who paints beautiful pictures with his right hand can, in a day and at the suggestion of a reporter, paint an equally good one with his left hand. The science of religion has a right to be heard scientifically through its qualified spokesmen, just as the science of physics or of astronomy has a right to be heard through its qualified spokesmen. Religion is a science despite the fact that some would make it only a sentiment.

Religion is not an open question, like the League of Nations, while science is a closed question, like the addition table. It has its principles, natural and revealed, which are more exacting in their logic than mathematics. But the false notion of tolerance has obscured this fact from the eyes of many who are as intolerant about the smallest details of life as they are tolerant about their relations to God.

In the ordinary affairs of life these same people would never summon a Christian Science practitioner to fix a broken window-pane; they would never call in an oculist because they had broken the eye of a needle; they would never call in a florist because they had hurt the palm of the hand, nor go to a carpenter to take care of their nails. They would never call in a Collector of Internal Revenue to extract a nickel swallowed by the baby. They would refuse to listen to a Kiwanis booster discussing the authenticity of an alleged Rembrandt, or to a tree-surgeon settling a moot question of law. And yet for the all-important subject of religion, on which our eternal destinies hinge, on the all-important question of the relations of man to his environment and to his God, they are willing to listen to any one who calls himself a prophet. And so our journals are filled with articles for these "broad-minded" people, in which every one from Jack Dempsey to the chief cook of the Ritz Carlton tells about his idea of God, and his view of religion. These same individuals, who would become exasperated if, in violation of a Watsonian fancy in education, their child played with a wrongly colored lollipop, would not become the least bit worried if he grew up without ever having heard the name of God.

Would it not be in perfect keeping with the fitness of things to insist on certain minimal requirements for theological pronouncements?

If we insist that he who mends our pipes know something about plumbing and that he who gives us pills know something about medicine, should we not expect and demand that he who tells us about God, religion, Christ, and immortality at least say his prayers? If Kreisler does not disdain to practise his scales, why should the modern theologian disdain to practise the elements of religion?

Another evidence of the breakdown of reason that has produced this weird fungus of broad-mindedness is the passion for novelty, as opposed to the love of truth. Truth is sacrificed for an epigram, and the Divinity of Christ for a head-line in the Monday morning newspaper. Many a modern preacher is far less concerned with preaching Christ and Him crucified than he is with his popularity with his congregation. A want of intellectual backbone makes him straddle the ox of truth and the ass of nonsense, paying compliments to Catholics because of "their great organization" and to sexologists because of their "honest challenge to the youth of this generation." Bending the knee to the mob and pleasing men rather than God would probably make them scruple at ever playing

100

the rôle of a John the Baptist before a modern Herod. No accusing finger would be leveled at a divorce or one living in adultery; no voice would be thundered in the ears of the rich, saying with something of the intolerance of Divinity: "It is not lawful for thee to live with thy brother's wife." Rather would we hear: "Friend, times are changing! The acids of modernity are eating away the fossils of orthodoxy. If thy noble sex-urge to self-expression finds its proper stimulus and response in no one but Herodias, then in the name of Freud and Russell accept her as thy lawful wife to have and to hold until sex do ye part."

Belief in the existence of God, in the Divinity of Christ, in the moral law, are considered passing fashions. The latest thing in this new tolerance is considered the true thing, as if truth were a fashion, like a hat, instead of an institution, like a head. At the present moment, in psychology the fashion runs towards Behaviorism, as in philosophy it runs towards Temporalism. And that it is not objective validity which dictates the success of a modern philosophical theory, is borne out by the statement a celebrated space-time philosopher of England made to the writer a few years ago, when he was asked where he got his system. "From my imagination," he answered. Upon being challenged that the imagination was not the proper faculty for a philosopher to use, he retorted: "It is, if the success of your philosophical system depends not on the truth that is in it, but on its novelty."

In that statement is the final argument for modern broad-mindedness: truth is novelty, and hence "truth" changes with the passing fancies of the moment. Like the chameleon who changes his colors to suit the vesture on which he is placed, so truth is supposed to change to suit the foibles and obliquities of the age, as if the foundations of thinking might be true for the pre-Adamites and false for the Adamites. Truth does grow, but it grows homogeneously, like an acorn into an oak; it does not swing in the breeze, like a weathercock. The leopard does not change his spots nor the Ethiopian his skin, though the leopard be put in bars or the Ethiopian in pink tights. The nature of certain things is fixed, and none more so than the nature of truth. Truth may be contradicted a thousand times, but that only proves that it is

102

strong enough to survive a thousand assaults. But for any one to say, "Some say this, some say that, therefore there is no truth," is about as logical as it would have been for Columbus, who heard some say, "The earth is round," and others say, "The earth is flat," to conclude: "Therefore there is no earth at all."

It is this kind of thinking that cannot distinguish between a sheep and his second coat of wool, between Napoleon and his three-cornered hat, between the substance and the accident, the kind that has begotten minds so flattened with broadness that they have lost all their depth. Like a carpenter who might throw away his rule and use each beam as a measuring-rod, so, too, those who have thrown away the standard of objective truth have nothing left with which to measure but the mental fashion of the moment.

The giggling giddiness of novelty, the sentimental restlessness of a mind unhinged, and the unnatural fear of a good dose of hard thinking, all conjoin to produce a group of sophomoric latitudinarians who think there is no difference between God as Cause and God as a "mental projection"; who equate Christ and

Buddha, St. Paul and John Dewey, and then enlarge their broad-mindedness into a sweeping synthesis that says not only that one Christian sect is just as good as another, but even that one world-religion is just as good as another. The great god "Progress" is then enthroned on the altars of fashion, and as the hectic worshipers are asked, "Progress towards what?" the tolerant answer comes back, "More progress." All the while sane men are wondering how there can be progress without direction and how there can be direction without a fixed point. And because they speak of a "fixed point," they are said to be behind the times, when really they are beyond the times mentally and spiritually.

In the face of this false broad-mindedness, what the world needs is intolerance. The mass of people have kept up hard and fast distinctions between dollars and cents, battle-ships and cruisers, "You owe me" and "I owe you," but they seem to have lost entirely the faculty of distinguishing between the good and the bad, the right and the wrong. The best indication of this is the frequent misuse of the terms "tolerance" and "intolerance." There are some minds that believe that intolerance is always wrong, because they make "intolerance" mean hate, narrow-mindedness, and bigotry. These same minds believe that tolerance is always right because, for them, it means charity, broad-mindedness, American good-nature.

What is tolerance? Tolerance is an attitude of reasoned patience towards evil, and a forbearance that restrains us from showing anger or inflicting punishment. But what is more important than the definition is the field of its application. The important point here is this: Tolerance applies only to persons, but never to truth. Intolerance applies only to truth, but never to persons. Tolerance applies to the erring; intolerance to the error.

What has just been said here will clarify that which was said at the beginning of this chapter, namely, that America is suffering not so much from intolerance, which is bigotry, as it is from tolerance, which is indifference to truth and error, and a philosophical nonchalance that has been interpreted as broad-mindedness.

Greater tolerance, of course, is desirable, for there can never be too much charity shown to persons who differ with us. Our Blessed Lord

105

Himself asked that we "love those who calumniate us, for they are always persons," but He never told us to love the calumny. In keeping with the Spirit of Christ, the Church encourages prayers for all those who are outside the pale of the Church, and asks that the greatest charity be shown towards them. As St. Francis de Sales was wont to say: "It is easier to catch flies with a drop of honey than with a barrel of vinegar."

If some of us who are blessed with its sacred privileges believed the same things about the Church that her slanderers believe, if we knew her only through the words of traitors or third-rate lies of dishonest historians, if we understood her only through those who were never cradled in her sacred associations, we would perhaps hate the Church just as much as they do. The bitterest enemies of the Church, those who accuse her of being unpatriotic, as Christ was accused of being before Pilate; of being unworldly, as Christ was accused of being before Herod; of being too dogmatic, as Christ was accused of being before Caiaphas; or being too undogmatic, as Christ was accused of being before Annas; of being possessed by the devil,

106

as Christ was accused of being before the Pharisees—these do not really hate the Church. They cannot hate the Church any more than they can hate Christ; they hate only that which they mistakenly believe to be the Catholic Church, and their hate is but their vain attempt to ignore.

Charity, then, must be shown to persons, and particularly to those outside the fold who by charity must be led back, that there may be one fold and one Shepherd.

Thus far tolerance, but no farther. Tolerance does not apply to truth or principles. About these things we must be intolerant, and for this kind of intolerance, so much needed to rouse us from sentimental gush, I make a plea. Intolerance of this kind is the foundation of all stability. The Government must be intolerant about malicious propaganda, and during the World War it made an index of forbidden books to defend national stability, as the Church, who is in constant warfare with error, makes her index of forbidden books to defend the permanency of Christ's life in the souls of men. The Government during the war was intolerant about the national heretics who refused to accept her principles concerning the necessity of democratic institutions, and took physical means to enforce such principles. The soldiers who went to war were intolerant about the principles they were fighting for, in the same way that a gardener must be intolerant about the weeds that grow in his garden. The Supreme Court of the United States is intolerant about any private interpretation of the first principle of the Constitution that every man is entitled to life, liberty, and the pursuit of happiness, and the particular citizen who would interpret "liberty" in even such a small way as meaning the privilege to "go" on a red traffic-light, would find himself very soon in a cell where there were no lights, not even the yellow—the color of the timid souls who know not whether to stop or go. Architects are as intolerant about sand as foundations for sky-scrapers as doctors are intolerant about germs in their laboratories, and as all of us are intolerant of a particularly broad-minded, "tolerant," and good-natured grocer who, in making our bills, adds seven and ten to make twenty.

Now, if it is right—and it is right—for governments to be intolerant about the principles of government, and the bridge-builder to be intolerant about the laws of stress and strain, and the physicist to be intolerant about the principles of gravitation, why should it not be the right of Christ, the right of His Church, and the right of thinking men to be intolerant about the truths of Christ, the doctrines of the Church, and the principles of reason? Can the truths of God be less exacting than the truths of mathematics? Can the laws of the mind be less binding than the laws of science, which are known only through the laws of the mind? Shall man, gifted with natural truth, who refuses to look with an equally tolerant eye on the mathematician who says two and two make five and the one who says two and two make four, be called a wise man, and shall God, Who refuses to look with an equally tolerant eye on all religions, be denied the name of "Wisdom," and be called an "intolerant" God?

Shall we say that the reflected rays of the sun are warm but the sun is not hot? This we are equivalently saying when we admit intolerance of the principles of science and deny it to the Father of science, Who is God. And if a government, with the inflexible principles of its constitution, distant from the foundation of government by miles and separated from it by lifetimes, can empower men to enforce that constitution, why cannot Christ choose and delegate men with the power of enforcing His Will and spreading His benedictions? And if we admit intolerance about the foundations of a government that at best looks after man's body, why not admit intolerance about the foundations of a government that looks after the eternal destiny of the spirit of man? For unlike human governments, "there is no other foundation upon which men can build than upon the name Jesus."

Why, then, sneer at dogmas as intolerant? On all sides we hear it said to-day, "The modern world wants a religion without dogmas," which betrays how little thinking goes with that label, for he who says he wants a religion without dogmas is stating a dogma, and a dogma that is harder to justify than many dogmas of faith. A dogma is a true thought, and a religion without dogmas is a religion without thought, or a back without a backbone. All sciences have dogmas. "Washington is the capital of the United States" is a dogma of geography.

"Water is composed of two atoms of hydrogen and one of oxygen" is a dogma of chemistry. Should we be broad-minded and say that Washington is a sea in Switzerland? Should we be broad-minded and say that H_2O is a symbol for sulphuric acid?

We cannot verify all the dogmas of science, history, and literature, and therefore we are to take many of them on the testimony of others. I believe Professor Eddington, for example, when he tells me that "Einstein's law of gravitation asserts that ten principal coëfficients of curvature are zero in empty space," just as I do not believe Dr. Harry Elmer Barnes when he tells me that "the cockroach has lived substantially unchanged on the earth for fifty million years." I accept Dr. Eddington's testimony because, by his learning and his published works, he has proved that he knows something about Einstein. I do not accept Dr. Barnes's testimony about cockroaches because he has never qualified in the eyes of the modern world as a cockroach specialist. In other words, I sift testimony and accept it on reason.

So also, my reason sifts the historical evidence for Christ; it weighs the testimony ad-

111

duced by those who knew Him, and the testimony given by Himself. It fails to be swayed by those who start with a preconceived theory, rejecting all the evidence against their theory and accepting the residue as the Gospels. In the search, it comes across such works as those of Renan and Strauss, which are critical, but it also comes across such works as those of Fillion and Grandmaison: it knows the name of Loisy, but it also knows Lagrange; it knows the theory of Inge, but it also knows D'Herbigny. And this reason finally leads me to accept the testimony of Jesus Christ as the testimony of God. I then accept these truths—truths which I cannot prove, as was Professor Eddington's statement about Einstein—and these truths become dogmas.

There can thus be dogmas of religion as well as dogmas of science, and both of them can be revealed, the one by God, the other by man. Not only that—these fundamental dogmas, like the first principles of Euclid, can be used as raw material for thinking, and just as one scientific fact can be used as the basis of another, so one dogma can be used as the basis for another. But in order to begin thinking on a first dogma, one must be identified with it either in time or in principle. The Church was identified with Christ in both time and principle; she began thinking on His first principles and the harder she thought, the more dogmas she developed. Being organic like life, not institutional like a club, she never forgot those dogmas; she remembered them and her memory is *tradition*. Just as a scientist must depend on the memory of the first principles of his science, which he uses as the ground for other conclusions, so too the Church goes back into her intellectual memory, which is tradition, and uses former dogmas as the foundation for new ones. In this whole process she never forgets her first principles. If she did she would be like the undogmatic dogmatists of the present day, who believe that progress consists in denying the fact, instead of building on it; who turn to new ideals because they have never tried the old; who condemn as "obscurantist" the truth that has a parentage, and glorify as "progressive" a shibboleth that knoweth not either its father or its mother. They are of the school that would deny the very nature of things: free the camel of his hump and call him a camel;

113

shorten the neck of a giraffe and call him a giraffe; and never frame a picture, because a frame is a limitation and therefore a principle and a dogma.

But it is anything but progress to act like mice and eat the foundations of the very roof over our heads. Intolerance about principles is the foundation of growth, and the mathematician who would deride a square for always having four sides, and in the name of progress would encourage it to throw away even only one of its sides, would soon discover that he had lost all his squares. So too with the dogmas of the Church, of science, and of reason; they are like bricks, solid things with which a man can build, not like straw, which is "religious experience," fit only for burning.

A dogma, then, is the necessary consequence of the intolerance of first principles, and that science or that church which has the greatest amount of dogmas is the science or the church that has been doing the most thinking. The Catholic Church, the schoolmaster for twenty centuries, has been doing a tremendous amount of solid, hard thinking and hence has built up dogmas as a man might build a house of brick

114

but grounded on a rock. She has seen the centuries with their passing enthusiasms and momentary loyalties pass before her, making the same mistakes, cultivating the same poses, falling into the same mental snares, so that she has become very patient and kind to the erring pupils, but very intolerant and severe concerning the false. She has been and she will always be intolerant so far as the rights of God are concerned, for heresy, error, untruth, affect not personal matters on which she may yield, but a Divine Right in which there is no yielding. Meek she is to the erring, but violent to the error. The truth is divine; the heretic is human. Due reparation made, she will admit the heretic back into the treasury of her souls, but never the heresy into the treasury of her wisdom. Right is right if nobody is right, and wrong is wrong if everybody is wrong. And in this day and age we need, as Mr. Chesterton tells us, "not a Church that is right when the world is right, but a Church that is right when the world is wrong."

The attitude of the Church in relation to the modern world on this important question may be brought home by the story of the two

115

women in the court-room of Solomon. Both of them claimed a child. The lawful mother insisted on having the whole child or nothing, for a child is like truth—it cannot be divided without ruin. The unlawful mother, on the contrary, agreed to compromise. She was willing to divide the babe, and the babe would have died of broad-mindedness.

THE PHILOSOPHY OF MEDIEVAL ART

THE PHILOSOPHY OF MEDIEVAL ART

THERE is no such thing as understanding art in any period apart from the philosophy of that period. Philosophy inspires art, and art reflects philosophy. We can never tell what the art of an age is unless we know what is the thought of the age. If the thought is lofty and spiritual, art will be lofty and spiritual; if the thought is base and material, art will be base and material. If the thought is of the heavens heavenly, art will be of the heavens heavenly; if the thought is of the earth earthly, art will be of the earth earthly. In that period of Grecian history, for example, when Plato and Socrates and Aristotle were giving eternal truths to men, the clear lines of the Parthenon and the airy Ionic of the Erechtheion served as so many petrified incarnations of their thought. Closer to our own times, when Rousseau set loose his exaltation of the ego and the romanticism of sense-passion, artists were found drinking at his fountain the shallow drafts of hatred for academic tradition, a license of inspiration, and a glorification of fleshy sensibilities. And now in our own day, what is the philosophical inspiration of Futurism and its wild love of novelty and "absolute commencements," motion for motion's sake, but the thought of Henri Bergson? What is the philosophical inspiration of Cubism, with its unrelated blocks, but the philosophy of Pluralism, which maintains that the multiple does not imply the unit? What is the whole inspiration of modern art but a Subjectivism introduced by Kant and his school, the heritage of which is a belief that no work of art itself is beautiful, but that it is our psychic or mental states that are beautiful, either because we project these states to the object, which is the *Einfühlung* theory, or because they harmonize with the tastes and commandments of society, which is the sociological theory, or because they produce interesting reactions, which is the Pragmatic theory?

If modern philosophy explains modern art, mediæval philosophy explains mediæval art. If we are to understand why they painted and why they sculptured and why they built a certain way, we must ask ourselves how they thought, for art is the lyrical expression of philosophy. Their civilization was much different from our own; in the thirteenth century Christendom knew but one Church. There was just one Faith, one Lord, one Baptism, one Church. Since it was one in its rule of faith, it is easy to extract those basic principles of mediæval life which served as the inspiration of their art. These principles are threefold: (1) Impersonalism, (2) Dogmatism, (3) Sacramentalism. Their thought was impersonal, and because it was impersonal, it was capable of being dogmatic, and all its dogmatism is summed up in its Sacramentalism. We shall expose these principles in contrast with modern principles, and then show how they worked themselves out in the art of that period.

Individualism is the characteristic of modern thought; impersonalism is the characteristic of mediæval thought. The egocentrism of modern thought has its roots in Descartes, who in his "Discourse on Method" expressed contempt for all history and insisted that all philosophy should be made a *tabula rasa* to be written on anew. Writing to Gassendi, he said: "You for-

121

get that you speak to a man who does not wish to know if any one ever existed before him; I, I, I, that is enough." Kant, the *privat-dozent* of Königsberg, did not suffer this individualism to die. His thought, he said, would be like a Copernican revolution in the world. Instead of the world's revolving about self and impressing itself on self, the self would revolve about the world and impress itself on the world. This egocentrism was carried to its limits in the philosophy of Pragmatism, which makes the individual the measure of truth. What is useful is true, according to Pragmatism. If God is useful for your life, He exists for you; if He is not useful for my life, He does not exist for me. The individual is all-important. Pragmatism was a war against Truth. Truth is not transcendental, it declared; it is ambulatory. It is personal and individual.

On the contrary, for the Scholastic or the mediævalist, truth is eternal and common. It is like a great edifice gradually built up from the accumulations of centuries. Like a great patrimony it passes from one generation to another and at no time is it considered *the personal property of him who finds it*. St.

Thomas Aquinas, the master mind of this period and perhaps the master mind of all times, insists on this impersonal constitution of truth. Referring to that great Greek thinker, Aristotle, whom he has dignified with the title "The Philosopher," he writes: "That which a single mind can bring, through his work and genius, to the promotion of truth is little in comparison with the total of knowledge. However, from all these elements, selected and coördinated and brought together, there arises a marvelous thing, as is shown by the various departments of learning, which by the work and sagacity of many minds have come to a wonderful augmentation."

Because truth was impersonal there was a great reverence for tradition in the Middle Ages. Tradition is not, as some believe, a heritage of the Dark Ages, something that cabins and confines thought; rather, it is a memory. A sense and an intellectual memory are indispensable conditions of all right thinking. We are under the necessity of going back to the storehouse of our mind for past impressions and thoughts in order to build up the present thought. What is true of the individual is true of society. Tradition is the memory of society and without that tradition society cannot think. "It is owing to tradition," says Pascal, "that the whole procession of men in the course of so many centuries may be considered as a single mind who always subsists and who learns continually."

Because truth is impersonal and the common patrimony of mankind, the great thinkers of that time rarely referred to another thinker by his own name. Run through the "Summa" of Aquinas or the works of any of the other great thinkers such as Richard of St. Victor, Bonaventure, and Scotus, and observe the frequency of such expressions as: *"Aliquis dicit,"* *"Unus dicit"* ("Some one says"; "They say"). St. Thomas, for example, in refuting the Anselmian a priori argument for the existence of God in the "Summa" does not mention Anselm's name, and although he and Bonaventure taught around the corner from each other there is no mention of the other in the writings of either. Neither does the Angelic Doctor mention even once the name of his teacher, Albertus Magnus, probably because he was enjoined by the humility of his master to keep it silent.

124

If thought is impersonal it will necessarily be dogmatic, that is, express itself in certain universal and general concepts. Here again there is a wide difference between the modern notion of dogma and the mediæval notion and the tradition that continues it. The modern notion is that truths change with the times; that just as we discard the old phaëton of our grandfathers for the limousine of the twentieth century, so too we change grandfather's notions of morality and religion for the modern notions. Scientific progress is said to have shown the futility of old dogmas, and the microscope is said to have revealed the inanities of theology.

For the mediævalist, on the contrary, dogmas are no more subject to change than the multiplication table. Two and two make four for the thirteenth century as well as for the twentieth, and a dogma like that of the Incarnation is as true for the twentieth as it is for the thirteenth century. Dogmas are above space and time because they are not sentimental appreciations of a sentimentalist, but intellectual truths of an intellect. Neither is theology a mere science of comparative religions. St. Thomas teaches that theology is the queen of

125

sciences, that "it surpasses all sciences in its principles, its object, its certitude, and its end." In theology everything possesses its own objective value; it is true in itself, apart from our appreciation of it. Its dogmas are not barriers to thought. They are no more confining for a mind than plan, contour, and choice of colors are confining for an artist. No great artist ever complained about the exigencies of dogma. A dogma is for the artist what the multiplication table is for the mathematician, or the logarithms are for the calculist, or the law of gravitation is for the physicist. They are not dams that wall up the river of thought; they are breakwaters that prevent it from overflowing the country-side of sanity.

Modern thinkers are quite generally prepared to look upon this world as a lasting city and as an end rather than as a means to an end. They quote Swinburne approvingly: "Glory to man in the highest, for man is the master of all." Religion then, instead of becoming the sum of man's duties toward God, becomes the sum of God's duties toward man. A typical expression of its nature is the following, "To put the question bluntly, religion

126

must be separated from the other-worldly pull of the traditional theologies and be sanely grounded in the outlook of modern knowledge." Earth must resume its rights, for the earth is the paradise and the end of man.

But in the perennial thought of the Scholastics, religion meant an ordination to God as our First Cause and Last End. Religion is no more intelligible without God than physics is intelligible without matter. The world, too, instead of being an end is a means to an end. In other words, the world is a great sacrament. There are seven sacraments in the supernatural order, which elevate and perfect man in the higher divine life, and in the natural order, everything can be a sacrament. A sacrament is a material thing used as a channel of spiritual sanctification, and since everything is destined to lead us to God, everything is a sacrament. The process by which matter is to be sacramentalized is after the fashion of a pyramid, at the base of which is the material order and at the peak of which is man. There is progress and continuity in the universe. Plants consume minerals, animals consume plants and minerals, and man consumes all three. Thus,

127

physically, there is within man the whole material universe.

But there is yet another way than the physical one by which he possesses all orders below him, and that is by knowledge. Because man has a spiritual soul he can know all things and thus contain all things within himself in a spiritual way. Hence man is destined to become not only a microcosm, as Aristotle tells us, but a living voice for all creation. He is to be the spokesman of the minerals, the plants, and the animals, for the very reason that he sums up all these orders. He is to lead them all back to God. The mineral cannot thank God for its creation but man can do so in the name of the mineral. Man thus becomes the bridge between the realm of brute matter and the realm of pure spirit. He is like unto matter inasmuch as he has a body and like unto pure spirit inasmuch as he has a soul. Standing midway between the two, he has been destined by God to be the mouthpiece of creation and to chant with the three youths in the fiery furnace a Benedicite to the Creator. Such was Sacramentalism as the Scholastics conceived it and as the Neo-Scholastics still conceive it. It is a system that

128

looks to the earth not as the forlorn hope of man but as the great channel of spiritualization, and regards the tawdry tinsel of this world's poor show as a stepping-stone to the tearless eternity of the heavenly Jerusalem.

Philosophy in the Middle Ages was impersonal, dogmatic, and sacramental. It was impersonal because truth was not the property of an individual; it was dogmatic because truth was above time and space; it was sacramental because the world was a stepping-stone to God. The art of this period was inspired by these thoughts and hence its three supreme characteristics are its impersonalism, its dogmatism, and its Sacramentalism.

The impersonal and eternal note is struck in every phase of the art of this period. Romances like the "Romance of the Rose"; Latin hymns like the *"Dies Iræ"* and those of the "Little Hours," have come down to us with little or no trace of the author who wrote them. The same must be said of the works of art. The rose windows of the Cathedral of Lincoln, pieces of which have come down to us, bear no trace of their maker. None of the illuminated manuscripts of the Bible or the missal or the breviary of this period are stamped with the name of the artist. Since many of these works were made in cloisters, it is likely that the rule of humility moved many of the artists to hide their names. As a matter of fact, it is one of the rules of the Benedictines that monks who work in monasteries shall produce works of art with great humility of spirit.

But the impersonal character is to be found in the Gothic system, which, says Dr. De Wulf, "resembles Scholastic philosophy and helps us to understand it. For the Gothic system is the property of every one; while each architect may interpret it in his own way, it belongs in reality to no one. Even now, we do not know the names of all those who conceived the plans and directed the work on the great cathedrals." And yet if our modern bridges and factories and smelting-plants survive four or five centuries, the generations of those days will know not only the name of the architect who designed them but even those of his assistants and the public officials of the time. Armies of sculptors chiseled the Virgins and the saints that occupy the portals and the niches, and yet how few of these have sealed their works with their names! The builders of the cathedrals, like Dante, were building for eternity; and in their minds, the materials of their structures were to survive for centuries; they were to last not for one generation but for all generations. Just as the thinkers of that time were hiding their identity because of the impersonality of truth and saying, *"Aliquis dicit,"* so too the artists of the time were hiding their identity in works of art that never betrayed the hand that held the chisel.

The reason of it all was that they were working for God. It mattered not for the mediæval artist how obscure the portion of the cathedral at which he was set, he decorated it as beautifully as he knew how, without a thought that his work would be appreciated only by the few who would see it. Trivial details were finished with all the perfection of important parts. Microscopic studies in recent years have revealed beautiful designs of pollen-grains and diatoms that are far beneath the possibilities of human vision. Always these beauties were there, though hidden from the naked eye. Whether men saw these details, or the fineness of the technique, or the beauty of inspiration matters little. God saw, and that was enough. Hence it is not surprising to find statues hidden in the tower of the Cathedral of Chartres that are just as perfect in detail as the statues above the door. Such impersonality in art could come only from a people who took a definite cognizance of the existence of God. The very silence of their work was an acknowledgment that their own artistry was from God and not from themselves. Why should their names be chiseled on stone when the gift of chiseling comes from God? Why should they cry out their own sufficiency when their whole being acknowledged their insufficiency? Why should they glorify themselves when only the glory of God mattered? Why should they care to leave their names to posterity as long as their names were written in the Book of Life? And thus we have the superb spectacle of the Angel Choir of Lincoln, which is said to be the most beautiful work ever dropped from the hand of man, coming down to our own day without even a hint or a record of those who designed and executed it. Truly there was only one thing necessary—*unum necessarium*—the glory of God.

132

A dogma for the Middle Ages was a conceptual expression of an eternal religious truth. Unlike the modern world, those men did not believe that dogmas change like the styles of clothes. They are eternal, because they are truths about the eternal and immutable God. Being eternal, they could be put in stone—a lasting substance—so that the twentieth century, for example, could have that truth brought to it by the thirteenth, and testify to the thirteenth the indefectibility of dogma. If the mediævalists had believed that dogmas were evolving they probably would have made their churches of gutta-percha, which could be fashioned to suit the whims of the changing centuries. The mediævalists had more in common with the pagans of the past than with the neo-pagans of the present. It was Plato who said beautifully, over three centuries before the coming of Christ: "The artist who fixes his eyes upon the unchanging beauty and uses it as a model in reproducing the idea of virtue can never fail to produce a work of finished beauty, while he who has his eyes fixed on the changing things of time and their perishable models can make nothing beautiful." And Cicero tells

133

us that Phidias "in making a Jupiter or a Minerva, did not have his eyes upon a particular model but upon a certain finished type of beauty which inspired his art and guided his hand." For all great artists dogmas of religion have been the inspiration of art. Religion is the foundation of art, says Rodin, and the essence of religion is dogma. The first poem is Genesis, the first architecture a Temple of God, and the first statue a deity. Like water rushing madly through narrow conduits that have no other outlet than from above, like the martyrs surrounded by the great hostile "thumbs-down" crowd of the Coliseum who had no means of escape but the open heavens above them, so too the soul cramped by the body seeks God as its outlet, pours out itself to Him to ravish itself with the ideal, to speak a language that enlightens, to carve and cut with the glorious liberty of the sons of God.

What are some of the dogmas that inspired the artists of those ages? If we are to judge by the works they have left us, any dogma sufficed to inspire them—the Trinity, the Incarnation, the Primacy of Peter, the Resurrection. From among them all we choose two that have been more or less forgotten or distorted by the modern age, namely, Future Life as depicted by the Gospel, and the cult of the Blessed Virgin Mary.

The mediævalists took the whole Gospel seriously and believed every word of it because they believed Him who gave testimony of the truth. When Christ said: "This is My Body, This is My Blood," they believed, and there was the dogma of the Eucharist. When Christ said to His Apostles and their successors: "Whose sins you shall forgive, they are forgiven them, and whose sins you shall retain, they are retained," they believed, and there was the dogma of Penance. When Christ said: "I am the Truth. . . . My Truth I give you," they believed, and there was the dogma of the Infallibility. When Christ said: "And the wicked shall be cast into everlasting fire with the devil and his angels," they believed, and there was the dogma of Eternal Hell.

The future life was something that was continually held up before the gaze of the mediævalist. It was appointed unto all men once to die and after that the judgment. Death is frequently represented in the cathedrals and

135

always with a fundamental optimism of making us reflect upon rather than fear death. In the beginning of the thirteenth century there flourished a poem that gave the key to much of the art of that period. It was called "The Dance of the Three Dead and the Three Living." Three young lords met one evening in the depths of an old cemetery. Three dead men appeared to them and each taught them a lesson: The first said, "I was Pope"; the second: "I was a Cardinal"; and the third: "I was the secretary of the Pope." Then all three said: "Look on us now; you will be just as we are now, power, honors, and riches count for nothing. At the moment of death it is only good works that count." This story took on a slightly different form but still is easily recognizable in the window, "The Triumph of Death," at Campo Santo of Pisa. The "Danse Macabre" in the Cathedral of Amiens was likewise inspired by it; it embraces all human conditions from the king to the peasant. One of the most horrible reminders of death is the skeleton in the Church of St. Peter of Bar le Duc, which is covered with a film of half-rotted flesh hanging over the bones like a faded drapery. It is

136

intended to produce a great feeling of insecurity in this life even in the moments when we are most wedded to it.

The Last Judgment finds its best expression in the central door of the Cathedral of Notre Dame of Paris. Christ is seated in His Majesty showing the wounds of His hands; beside Him is the cross with which He has conquered death, and round about Him are the Blessed Virgin and angels. In a lower panel angels are going forth to the four corners of the earth and the utmost bounds of them with trumpets summoning the dead to rise to judgment. The just are signed with the Tau, the cross, and are placed on the right; the unjust are placed on the left and bound with ropes to be cast into utter darkness.

Heaven was represented as the heavenly Jerusalem descending from the sky, or else symbolically as the bosom of Abraham, such as we see it over the north door of Rheims Cathedral. Hell is represented by demons of hideous shapes, but best of all by a petrification of the words that Dante tell us are inscribed over hell, "All ye abandon hope who enter here." It was just such titanic glooms of the hopeless

137

that inspired Fra Angelico's representation of Hell.

One of the favorite dogmas that inspired mediæval art was the part of the Virgin Mary in the rôle of the redemption of the human race. It may be well to recall this dogma to those who are not familiar with it. There is a parallel between the Fall and the Redemption of man. Four elements contributed to the Fall: a disobedient man, Adam; a proud woman, Eve; a tree; and the fruit of the tree. Four elements contributed to our redemption: An obedient God-man, Jesus Christ; a humble woman, the Virgin Mary; a tree, the Cross; and the fruit of the Tree, Christ and the Eucharist. As the human race fell through a woman it was fitting that it should be redeemed through a woman. Mary is more than a mere accident in the reparation of the human race, and is represented as something more, namely, as the Mother of God. Never is she depicted with a passing charm or a seducing femininity or as a fleshly thing that might be set to the music of Massenet, but always with the freshness and perfume and virginity of the Mother of God. On the west side of the Cathedral of Amiens

138

there is a statue of her holding the Infant Who holds the world; under her feet is a devil being crushed by her heel, thus testifying that complete enmity would be placed between her and the devil, as foretold by Genesis—and acknowledged to-day in the dogma of the Immaculate Conception. Above the west door of the Cathedral of Paris there is a magnificent representation of her death and her coronation in Heaven, a subject that later on inspired Fra Angelico. In the Louvre hangs the famous painting wherein the Virgin is seated at the right hand of the Son in the triumph of her maternity. *"Astitit regina a dextris tuis, in vestitu de aurato."* In the center of the composition is Christ upon a throne, holding in both hands a crown, which He is placing on the head of His Mother. She kneels before Him, her hands folded across her breast. Around the throne are twenty-four angels singing her praises. Near them are saints of the Old and the New Testament, the very expression of whose visages testifies to the most pure and ineffable joy. Indeed Angelico understood what St. Thomas wrote of her beauty: "It purified the senses without in the least troubling them."

139

That this dogma of the Blessed Mother was once near and dear to the hearts of the mediævalists, as it is to those who continue that tradition to-day, is evidenced by the number of churches dedicated in her honor. The Cathedral of Paris—Notre Dame—is one of the most glorious of these testimonials to Our Lady. Throughout the whole mediæval empire and throughout England, cathedrals, shrines, and chapels were built in her name. In England there was such a devotion to her that England became known as "Mary's dowry" or "Mary's England," which our modern world has corrupted to Merry England—as if it could be merry without Mary. And of all the sad visions that drop before a traveler in Europe to-day there are none more sad than ruins of the Lady chapels. During the English Reformation, and under the leadership of Cromwell, four hundred monasteries and churches were destroyed. Statues of the Blessed Virgin and other saints were reduced to dust by the hammers beating out a new civilization. The barren niches of Lincoln Cathedral, the decapitated statues of York, and the white-washed Lady chapel of

Ely are so many sad vestiges to-day of that break with tradition.

In brief, the art of the Middle Ages is the art of a redeemed humanity. It is planted in the Christian soul at the border of living waters and under the Heaven of theological virtues and among the sweet zephyrs of the seven gifts of the Holy Ghost. For the Middle Ages there was no such thing as *making* Christian art. It was rather a matter of *being* a Christian. If you were a Christian, your art would be Christian. If you believed in eternal dogmas, your art would express eternal truth. Horace said, "If you wish me to weep, you must weep first," and the mediævalist said, "If you wish to carve the things of Christ, you must live with Christ." Art for the mediævalist demanded calm and meditation rather than hectic rush and excitement. History records that Fra Angelico wept while painting the "Crucifixion" that stands to-day in the Convent of San Marco in Florence.

The sacramental philosophy of the Middle Ages insisted that man is the center of the visible universe and that his life's mission is to lead creatures back to God. This Sacramentalism expressed itself in the art of the period, in making the cathedral the center of the political and social life of the time. Just as the religio-political life of the period converged towards the cathedral, so geographically the material structure of the city converged toward it. The Cathedral of Toledo, for example, is almost smothered by the structures that cling around it. It was foreign to the mind of the mediævalist to set the church off at a distance as if to magnify its beauty. Like to a mother who is surrounded by her children, who frolic like sheep about her, so too the cathedral welcomed the homes and drew them to her bosom. It was not distant and fearful admiration it solicited, but confidence and love. Like a mighty ocean greyhound ready for its voyage, the whole city seemed to embark within its flanks.

Just as the cathedral was the center of the political and social life of the time, so the Real Presence was the center and soul of the cathedral. As man, the microcosm, summed up all visible creation within himself, whose vital principle was a soul, so too the cathedral summed up all creation within itself, and its soul was the Eucharistic Emmanuel. The world is a great sacrament and the cathedral is a still greater one. The cathedral synthetized everything. All kingdoms, the mineral, the vegetable, the animal, the human, and the angelic—all arts, all sciences, all times—left their trace on it. All nature rebelled with Adam and all nature was redeemed with Christ. Hence Our Lord, when he sent out His Apostles to teach, did not say "Preach the Gospel to every man," but "Preach the Gospel to every creature." The architects of the cathedrals again took Him at His word and brought every creature into their structures; there are trees and flowers and birds and fishes. There are statues of cows on the top of the Cathedral of Laon, and vegetables over the door of the Cathedral of Rheims.

And the principle that unifies these things, what was it? Not a city like Mecca; not an organ or a pulpit, but God amongst men—not the mere abstract Great Architect of the Universe, nor a pantheistic equation with the world, but God mysteriously living under the appearance of Bread. There is a real heart palpitating in this sacramental universe of the cathedral and that heart is the Sacred Heart in the real sacrament of the Eucharist. This Divine Life bound together like a hoop of steel the various hierarchies of creation found therein. It did more than that; it revealed to the worshipers that great procession of life— Divine Life—that passes from Father to Son in the Trinity, from Son to human nature in the Incarnation, and from the Incarnation to us in the Eucharist, and which finally, to complete the circle, is some day to lead us back to God. "All are yours, you are Christ's, and Christ is God's." The Gothic cathedral, which is the philosophy of the Middle Ages in stone—can we ever forget it?

"Far away and long ere we catch the first view of the city itself," says Reinach, "the three spires of the Cathedral, rising above the din and turmoil, preach to us the Most High and Undivided Trinity. As we approach, the transepts striking out crosswise tell us of the Atonement. The Communion of Saints is set forth by the chapels clustering around the choirs and nave: the mythical weathercock bids us to watch and pray and endure hardness; the hideous forms that are seen hurrying from

the eaves speak the misery of those who are
cast out of the church; spire, pinnacle, and
finial, the upward curl of the sculptured foliage, the upward spring of the flying buttresses,
the sharp rise of the window arch, the high-
thrown pitch of the roof, all these overpower-
ing the horizontal tendency of string course
and parapet, teach us that vanquishing earthly
desires, we also should ascend in mind and
heart. Lessons of holy wisdom are written in
the delicate tracery of the windows; the unity
of many members is shadowed forth by the
multiplex arcade; the duty of letting our light
shine before men, by the pierced and flowered
parapet that crowns the whole."

We enter. The triple breadth of the nave
and aisles, the triple height of pier-arch, tri-
forium, and clerestory, the triple length of
choir, transepts, and nave, again set forth the
HOLY TRINITY. And what besides is there that
does not tell of our Blessed Saviour, that does
not point out HIM FIRST in the western door;
HIM LAST in the distant altar; HIM MIDST in
the great rood; HIM WITHOUT END in the mono-
gram carved on boss and corbel, in the Holy
Lamb, in the Lion of the Tribe of Judah, in

the mystic Fish? Close by us is the font, for
by regeneration we enter the Church; it is deep
and capacious, for we are buried in Baptism
with CHRIST; it is of stone, for He is the rock;
and its spiry cover teaches us, if we be indeed
risen from its waters with Him, to seek those
things which are above. Before us in long-
drawn vista are the massy piers, which are the
Apostles and Prophets—they are each of many
members, for many are the graces in every
saint; there is beautiful delicate foliage around
the head of all, for all were plentiful in good
works. Beneath our feet are the badges of
worldly pomp and glory, the graves of kings
and nobles and knights—all in the presence
of God as dross and worthlessness. Through
the walls wind the narrow cloister galleries,
emblems of the path by which the Church's
holy monks and anchorites, whose conflicts
were known only to their God, have reached
their home. And we are compassed about with
a mighty cloud of witnesses; the rich deep glass
of the windows teems with saintly forms, each
in its own fair niche, all invested with the same
holy repose; there are the glorious company
of the Apostles, the goodly fellowship of the

Prophets, the noble army of martyrs, the shining band of confessors, the jubilant chorus of virgins. There are kings who have long since changed an earthly for a heavenly crown, and bishops who have given in a glad account to the Shepherd and Bishop of souls. But on none of these things do we rest; piers, arch behind arch; windows, light behind light; arcades, shaft behind shaft; the roof, bay behind bay; the saints around us; the Heavenly Hierarchy above with dignity of preëminence still increasing eastward—each and all lead eye and soul and thought to the image of the Crucified Saviour as it glows in the great east window. Gazing steadfastly on, we pass up the nave, that is, through the Church Militant, till we reach the rood-screen, the barrier between it and the Church Triumphant, and therein shadowing forth the death of the faithful. High above it hangs on His triumphant CROSS the image of HIM Who by His death hath overcome death; on it are portrayed saints and martyrs, His warriors, who fighting under their Lord have entered into rest and inherit a tearless eternity. They are to be our examples, and the seven lamps above them typify those

147

graces of the SPIRIT by Whom alone we can tread in their steps. The screen itself glows with gold and crimson; with crimson, for they passed the Red Sea of martyrdom to obtain them. And through the delicate network, and the unfolding holy doors, we catch faint glimpses of the chancel beyond. There are the massy stalls, for in Heaven is everlasting rest; there are the sedilia, emblems of the seats of the Elders round the Throne; there is the piscina, for they have washed their robes and made them white; and there, heart and soul and life of all, the altar with its unquenchable lights, and golden carvings, and mystic steps, and sparkling jewels; even CHRIST Himself, by whose merits only we find admission to our heavenly inheritance. Verily, as we think on the oneness of its design, we may say, *"Jerusalem, quæ ædificatur ut civitas cujus participatio ejus in idipsum."*

Such is the cathedral as the great incarnation of mediæval thought. It is the invisible in the visible, the mystic in the historical, the spiritual in the carnal, the eternal in the temporal; it forms a new Eve taken from the universe as from an open side. In it, the Virgin

Cathedral, the Incarnate God makes His dwelling. It is the simple comprehension of the Person of Christ: *Ecce Homo*. The faithful who live there—that is humanity. Its vault is the sky; its walls with its windows, the horizon; the flaming rose window, the sun; its space, the atmosphere; and its very incompleteness—for few of the cathedrals have been completely finished—shows forth that human nature has higher ideals than it can attain by itself and that the completeness of things is never attained in this life but only in the world to come.

THE LYRICISM OF SCIENCE

THE LYRICISM OF SCIENCE

JUST as hidden in the strata of the earth there are fossils of prehistoric animals that survive from age to age, so, too, there are philosophical fossils hidden in the strata of university class-rooms and between the pages of magazine covers.

In the middle of the last century, the general spirit of the times was that of Positivism, Agnosticism, and Skepticism, which held that science was omniscient, and that a day would come when science would build babies in laboratories, and foretell the split second when the cross would supplant the crescent on the dome of St. Sophia. In cultured, refined, and truly scientific minds, this tendency to adore science has long since passed away. But a few fossils remain, and strange to relate, many of these fossils are described as "living philosophers," despite the fact that the philosophy that they present has been long dead. A typical statement chosen out of dozens, and representative of their attitude, is this: "The method we term 'scientific,' forms for the modern man the sole dependable means of disclosing the realities of existence. It is the sole authentic mode of revelation."

This idea that experience constitutes the sum of knowledge, that the scientific method is the only method of knowledge, that a belief in authority is due to "incompetence to cope with experience," that a thoroughgoing philosophy must be "framed in the light of science and technique," is nothing more than the antiquated philosophy of Auguste Comte and the more antiquated religious philosophy of Draper and White.

This attitude towards science is unscientific, and is nothing more than a survival attitude of the distorted mentality of the nineteenth century. There is not a single distinguished philosopher of science in the world to-day who believes in the fossil mentality that the scientific method is the only method of knowledge. In the litany of scientists, such men might be mentioned as Duhem, Meyerson, Poincaré, Milhaud, Boutroux, Dingler, Renoirte, Whitehead, Richardson, Millikan, whose position could be summed up in these words: The scientist does not seek the ultimate, but the proximate; he does not speak of the last analysis, but the next approximation. All these distinguished thinkers say that science is concerned only with the description of phenomena, or of *how* things take place, but not with the explanation of phenomena, or *why* they take place. Natural laws for them are descriptions of events, but nothing more. Science describes in terms of mathematics, but it does not explain in terms of causes. It has nothing to say about the real nature of things, but only elucidates certain relations between them.

I know it is dangerous to talk about the limitations of science, for one is liable to be put down as an obscurantist and a mediævalist, because science is supposed to be to certain minds something about which there is no dispute, like the multiplication table, while religion is supposed to be something that admits of dispute, like a disarmament conference. But in the light of the testimony of the distinguished scientists mentioned above, a few general points concerning the value of science may make our meaning clear:

155

1. Science is not inimical to a Christian civilization, for it has flourished only in a Christian civilization. It has not flourished in a Buddhist civilization, nor amongst the Mohammedans, for the reason that a pantheistic civilization that confuses God and the world can never get hold of the world alone to study it scientifically. The Christian conception, on the contrary, makes God and the world distinct, and therefore makes it possible for a man to study the universe as the universe. In doing this, man follows out the injunction of the Creator, Who commanded man to rule over the earth and subject it.

2. What has our great scientific advance in recent years done for us except to give us greater measurement, and great accuracy in the measurement, of secondary causes? Science is necessarily concerned only with secondary causes, like matter, light, force, electricity, but not with the primary cause, which is God. What is the essential difference between the old Greek theory that the world was made of four elements—air, earth, fire, and water—and the modern scientific theory that it is made up of electrical energy diversified into ninety-

156

two elements? Really, the only difference is a difference in the exactness of measurement, not a difference in interpretation of the whole. As Professor Whitehead tells us, the great scientific advance of the last fifty years is only an advance in the instruments of technique or measurement, but not in a knowledge of causes. The old Greeks measured crudely in yards; we measure skilfully in millimeters. They called things "chunks of matter," we call them "electrical charges." This certainly is an advance in the delicacy of measurement, but it is not necessarily an advance in the final explanation of things in terms of the First Cause, Which is God.

3. Science, according to modern philosophers of science, is concerned only with the observation of facts and their description in terms of mathematics, not with their explanation in terms of causes. Now it is quite true that, thanks to finer instruments, our *knowledge of facts* is better than that of the ancients, but our *interpretation* or explanation is not necessarily better. Thanks to our instruments, the modern eyes that see the heavens, and search the behavior of protons and electrons, are bet-

ter than the eyes of Aristotle, who had not these instruments. But it does not follow that our brains are any better than the brains of Aristotle. In this century, we know far more about microbes and galactic systems than did any of the mediæval philosophers, but I am not so sure that there is any mind to-day quite so capable of interpreting these facts as the mind of that great mediævalist, St. Thomas Aquinas. It is one thing to observe facts, another thing to interpret them. Facts as facts mean nothing; experience as experience means nothing. A cat walking through a laboratory sees the test-tubes and retorts just as well as the scientist—in fact sees them better in the dark. But the cat can make no conclusions concerning the facts, simply because it lacks the power of reason. It is reasoning on experience, then, that makes interpretation, and therefore I say that we are no better equipped to-day to interpret facts than the ancients were; we have only better facts to interpret.

4. There is danger that the ceaseless practice of exact measurement may dull the brain; hence minds that are excessively bent on observing tiny facts, formulating temporary hy-

potheses to describe those facts, may sooner or later come to despise or lose the lofty use of reason. The constant analyzing of things, tearing things into bits and labeling each, has spoiled our power of synthesis and our capacity to rise above or beyond measurement. Measurement is necessary, it is true, but a man could go mad thinking out the height of the Chrysler Building in terms of inches, though he would not go mad thinking it out in terms of stories. The Divine Wisdom once reminded us of the limitations of measurement and the impossibility of substituting measurement for cause: "What man by taking thought can add to his stature one cubit?"

5. It is untrue to say that the scientific method is "the sole authentic mode of revelation"; this statement is not only something unscientific, but it is also painful nonsense. The method of science is not the only method of knowledge. The claim is that it has produced what might be called "the lyricism of science." By this is meant the attitude that philosophy and theology should dance to the tune piped for it by the science enjoying popularity at the moment. Four distinct phases of this lyricism

159

of science during the past hundred years are noticeable, namely, the sociological, the biological, the psychological, and finally the physical. When Comte brought sociology to the fore the lyricists of the day, bent on making religion scientific, asked that religion, God, the supernatural, and Christianity be interpreted in terms of sociology. The ragged remnant of this school survives in those who make God sociological and define him as nothing but "society divinized."

Lyricism took a new life with the publication of Darwin's "Origin of Species," which purported to be nothing more than a purely scientific work. The lyricists of science insisted, however, that Darwin had changed the essence of religion and that from henceforth God and religion were to be lyricized in terms of biology. Religion then was explained as a slow evolution from animism or magic or fear to its present highly developed form of Christianity. God gave way to "the idea of God," the evolution of which idea was traced by the now forgotten Grant Allen, a man whose lyricism nevertheless has been swallowed whole by all those who insist on overhauling the idea of

God and of religion, to make them conform to its present-day evolved state in the biological unfolding of the universe.

At the beginning of this century a new science came into vogue with Professor James and Professor Meyers, namely, psychology, and with it a new lyrical theology that explained conversions as an explosion of subconscious states, defined God as a "mental projection," and at times reduced religion to a sex libido. This group of lyricizers produced such definitions of religion as this one from Ohio State University, "Religion is a projection in the roaring loom of time of a concentration or unified complex of psychical values." All of which goes to prove that for such minds, religion is something that they have got hold of, instead of being something that has got hold of them.

But these lyricisms are passé. The sociological, biological, and psychological lyricisms of science still survive, but the really modern theologians are those who plead for a revision of God and religion in terms of the recent discoveries in physics. Even the great Dr. Alfred N. Whitehead, one of the first-class scientists of whom our American universities can boast, after having written an excellent scientific work on "Science and the Modern World," followed it up with a theology entitled "Religion in the Making," wherein he gives to the world another sorry example that a man may be a very good scientist and yet a very poor theologian. This new lyrical group makes God the "harmony of epochal occasions," or else a "creature of the matrix space-time." God is not; He becomes. Deity is "a variable quality, and as the world grows in time deity changes with it." In the beginning was not the Word, but in the beginning was space-time. Time is with space and space is with time. Deity comes from this combination, and religion "is the duty of helping to create God's deity." In connection with this new physico-religion of space-time, one cannot help remarking that space supporting time, and time supporting space, as the ground of the universe, reminds one of the story of two men shipwrecked on an island who supported themselves by taking in each other's washing.

Why should it be the supreme right of physics, for example, to tell us what religion is?

Why should God be interpreted in terms of the theory of relativity, which belongs to the domain of physics, any more than by the discovery of insulin, which belongs to the domain of medicine? The method and content of one science is not the method and content of any other science. Just as the subject or predicate of one sentence cannot be transferred to another sentence, so neither can the categories of one science be transferred, without correction, to the categories of another science.

Because life evolves, it does not follow that God evolves. If the laws of psychology are not applicable to the facts of astronomy, and if the laws of music are not transferrable to engineering, and if the predicates of an amœba are not applicable to the Parthenon, why should the method of experimental science be applicable to the whole field of wisdom, even religion? Oxygen or hydrogen cannot be studied in the same way as justice and fortitude. Prohibition may be a "noble experiment," but it does not follow that individual liberty is also an experiment. Original sin is not to be studied in the same way as the electron, nor the fall of man in the same way as the

163

fall of an apple. Injustice, unkindness, and evil are not to be studied or known in just the same way as sulphuric acid. There is no such thing as putting a law-breaker into a crucible and stewing him until the unmistakable green fumes of lawlessness arise. It is one thing to be a relativist in physics and another thing to be a relativist in theology. Relativity may be true for the spheres, but it is being carried too far when it says that we have four fingers on one hand counted one way and six on the other counted another way; or when it says that from an airplane an uncle looks like an aunt. There is danger that a scientific method, if isolated, will go to one's head in the same way that wine does when taken on an empty stomach.

A PRE-FACE TO MORALS

WHEN one has read one book on morals by any "new" thinker of our day, he has read them all. Two dominant ideas run through each of them: the first is the decay of old traditions through the advance of modern culture; the second is a plea for a new morality suitable to the way men live to-day. The first argument is generally couched in some such language as this: "We do not live in a patriarchal society. We do not live in a world that disposes us to believe in a theocratic government. And therefore in so far as moral wisdom is entangled with the promises of a theocracy, it is unreal to me. It is the unconscious assumption that we are related to God as creatures to a creator, as vassals to a king, as children to a father, that the acids of modernity have eaten away." All these things have ceased to be consistent with our normal experience of ordinary affairs. Men no longer believe seriously that they are governed from Heaven, and anarchy will result

167

from all this confusion unless by conscious effort they find ways of governing themselves.

The second part of these books is generally consecrated to the elevation of Humanism to a system of morals. Starting with the premise that the history of every man is a history of his progress from infantilism to maturity, they conclude that a goal for moral effort can be found in the notion of maturity. "To replace the conception of man as the subject of a heavenly king, which dominates the ancestral order of life, humanism takes as its dominant pattern the progress of the individual from helpless infancy to self-governing maturity."

Maturity, then, is the goal of morals, and a successful passage from childhood to maturity means a breaking up and reconstruction of those habits which were appropriate only to our earliest experience. For example, when a childish disposition is carried over into an adult environment the result is a false valuation of that environment. The child-pattern is not the ideal. All this is another way of saying that when we become men we put away the things of a child. An infant knows neither vice nor virtue because it can respond only to that

168

which touches it immediately. A man has virtue in so far as he can respond to a larger situation. "To have virtue then is to respond to larger situations and to longer stretches of time and without much interest in their immediate result in convenience or pleasure. It is to overcome the impulses of immaturity, to detach oneself from objects that preoccupy it and from one's own preoccupations." Morality, then, for the individual will be procured by working for society or the commonwealth. Each man will be supposed to adjust his will to the will of others instead of trusting to custom and organic loyalties. The individual will learn to crush his selfish nature by looking to the good of humanity, of which he is a part.

As the ideal of maturity as the goal of morals unfolds itself, new labels are found, such as "maturity," "detachment," and "disinterestedness," all names for the goal of Humanistic morality or "high religion," which "will untangle the moral confusion of the ego and make plain what we are really driving at in our manifold activity."

What is to be thought of this type of book? Two general criticisms occur to us, one referring to the section that deals with the "modernity" of the modern mind, the other referring to the second section, which treats of the new morals of "disinterestness" or "maturity." We should say that the first part on the modern mind is too unmodern, and of the second part, that on the morals of "maturity," that it is too immature and the morals of "disinterestedness" are too selfish. When it is argued that the modern man can no longer live under the ancestral morality and the theocratic religions, and that a new morality must be found for him, one is really stating something very old and ancient. There are new men in the world, but there is still the "old man," in the sense that human nature has not changed. All such an author has done is to develop a man's lip-worship, or better still, to reburnish the Golden Calf.

Once upon a time, long before there were twentieth-century Modernists, Moses went up into the mountain to pray, and there he remained forty days and nights conversing with God. Now the people who were below—the really progressive people, who knew the thrill of fleshpots—became impatient with the authority of Moses and the ancestral idea of a Sovereign God, and so they besought Aaron, saying: "Make us gods that may go before us. For as to this Moses, the man that brought us out of the land of Egypt, we know not what has befallen him." This is the first part of the modern plea expressed in different words. What difference is there, except that of language? What difference is there between saying, "We know not what has befallen him" and, "The acids of modernity have melted away ancestral morality"? But to continue the story.

And so the people brought together their earrings and precious stones, and Aaron made for them a Golden Calf before which they fell down adoring, saying: "These are thy gods, O Israel, that have brought thee out of the land of Egypt," and they began in their maturity to become "disinterested" and "detached" from the God of Moses and wedded to the calf of Apis. Again, I must say there is little difference between Aaron's gathering a gold ring here and a gold earring there and melting them into a calf, and a modern Aaron's gathering a fragment from a psychologist here and a lesser fragment from a Freudian there, and fusing them into a modern Golden Calf called, say, "A Preface to Morals," and saying, "These are the gods that will bring us out of the darkness of old faiths and older creeds."

This reflection is passed apart from the intrinsic worth of the new morals advocated, which we shall pass on later. It is stated only to emphasize the truth that there are no "acids of modernity"; acids are what they were from the beginning of the world, whether they be sulphuric acid or the acid of skepticism. There is no such thing as modernity in thought; there is only antiquity with new labels, like new advertisements. Modernity belongs only to the world of mechanics, but there is nothing new in the world of morals. From the fall of the angels up until the crack of doom there have been and will be only two moral systems possible: one is to live the way we think, the other is to think the way we live. The latter has always been called the "modern" and the other the "ancient" or "ancestral," but the modernity is only a matter of new tags and new labels and not one of new enthusiasms. Speaking of tags, singular is the new label entitled

172

"high religion." We have had "high adventures," "high hats," "high Anglicanism," "high-balls"—now we have "high religion." Metaphors from Alpine climbers only becloud the issue. If writers who use such metaphors cared for directness, honesty, and outspokenness, they would not say that "ancestral morality" is too antiquated; they would say it is too hard! Such complaints against traditional morality have done nothing new except give the complaint against Moses a "new complexion" in the sense that modern beauty-specialists advertise, "Which complexion will you wear to-day?" But they have not given it a new face—they have merely given a new label to an old error. That is probably why such a work should be entitled "A Pre-face to Morals."

There is one fundamental criticism we would make of the morality of "maturity," and that is its immaturity; and one criticism of the morality of "disinterestedness," and that is its selfishness. It is well to remember that there are two kinds of maturity: physical maturity and spiritual maturity. Physical maturity is the full-orbed development of either the human organism or the body corporate in its material goings and comings. Spiritual maturity, however, is the perfection of spiritual faculties and the realization of all their tendencies and inclinations. The new morals provide for physical maturity in the sense that man, in his social relation with other men, is equipped with a principle that will enable him to reduce conflict, discord, and friction with other men to a minimum. Petty desires, which sometimes spoil the devoted scientist, selfish interests, which endanger social intercourse—all these are fairly well taken care of by a maturity of disinterestedness. But this is only a maturity of the material things round about us—men, affairs, business, social life. It is not a maturity about the things of the mind.

What provision does such a system make for the maturing of a mind which desires a love that does not end when a cold clod falls upon the object loved, but a love that is abiding and eternal; what provision does it make for the maturing of a mind that desires a truth which is not fragmentary like one found at the lower end of a microscope or the upper end of a telescope, but a truth that is pregnant with the

174

intelligibility of the mysteries of life and death; what provision does it make for the maturing of a mind which craves for a life that never passes the last embrace from friend to friend, or crumbles the last cake at life's great feast, but a life ever throbbing and aglow with eternal heart-beats? No morality is moral that matures man only in his social relations and in his physical wants and leaves unnourished and underfed and embryonic those ideals which differentiate him from the animals and the stars. It tells us how we may grow mature physically, but it has left us as unguided children so far as spiritual maturity is concerned. It is a morality for the finite reaches of our body, but not for the spiritual reaches of our soul; it supplies a maturity for the man who goes to bed, eats, drinks, plays golf, attends conferences, reads newspapers, buys and sells, but it does not supply a maturity for the man who thinks thoughts beyond these things, who has remorse of conscience, who wonders what is beyond the stars, and who sits up nights pondering on truth and justice.

The goal of this morality is the clock and the calendar. It is the maturity that leads to overripeness, then mellowness, then death, then dissolution. And the most striking proof that it has not given a thought to the maturity of the spirit is that it applies the notion of maturity of the body only to the Standard Oil Company, the Senate, and sex—business, government, and marriage. In the cold pedestrian language of everyday life, that kind of morals can be summed up in this injunction: "Unless you become as old men, you cannot enter into the Kingdom of Heaven." It might have been well for it to have considered more at length a Man Who gave a religion and a morality based upon the paradox of the maturity of infancy, and which startled men out of physical maturity when He said: "Unless you become as little children, you cannot enter the Kingdom of Heaven."

Finally, the morals of "disinterestedness" are too selfish. By salvaging from the wreck of Christianity the doctrine of detachment, one can build up a system of morals that shows the individual the way out of individual selfishness but not the way out of *social* selfishness. It is all very true to say that "disinterestedness" in self is accomplished by greater concern for the social group, but what will free man from selfishness for the social group? It is all very well to free man from individual pettiness, but who will free him from social pettiness? This modern morality might be compared to a father who, being anxious to escape the inheritance-tax by an act of "disinterestedness," gives his property to his sons while he is living, only thereby to fall into the sin of group-selfishness.

Why, it may be asked, is such a moral system socially selfish? For the same reason that its individual morality is free from individual selfishness, namely, because it looks out to the good of something outside itself, namely, the good of the social group. Now how can the social group or society be freed from social selfishness? Only by looking out to a goal outside of society, or, in other words, by beginning to be disinterested in itself. When Our Divine Lord said: "Be not solicitous for your life, what you shall eat, nor for your body, what you shall put on," He was not stating only a moral doctrine. He was enunciating a principle of perfectly good hygiene. He was saying that the only way to develop self is to forget self; that the only way to grow physically mature is to think of other things besides halitosis, fallen arches, and pyorrhea, or better still to be "disinterested" in these things, and to look out to something outside self. Now thus far the new morality is perfectly sound: Interest in the group is the cure for individual selfishness.

Now, why should not the same principle hold for the group? To say that the group must be interested in itself is to say that the group must be selfish, for the common good is really common to all the members. If there is to be such a thing as "social disinterestedness," then the group, or society, must begin to think of other things besides itself, and one of those things is what Pilate thought about for many days until his death: "There is no power given to you except from above." To work truly for the good of society, one must be carried away by enthusiasm for something outside society. Humanism of itself is insufficient. Detachment from the individual can be accomplished by attachment to society, but detachment from society can be accomplished only by attachment to God. For this reason there never was enunciated a principle better destined to affect social disinterestedness than that of Him Who said: "Seek ye first the Kingdom of God and His justice and all these things will be added unto you."

Such a morality is good so far as it goes, but it does not go far enough. It explains bodily maturity but not spiritual maturity: it escapes individual selfishness but not social selfishness, and the reason is the same in both cases—it has refused to anchor outside of the ship in which it is sailing. It is not a bad moral system; it is a truncated system, not yet grown to its full stature, immature with the immaturity of dwarfishness, and disinterested in the perfect development of man's noblest qualities. It will probably do much for those who do not want morals in the strict sense of the term. It will be a temporary morality for a few select Humanists, but it will never be a morality for humanity: it will explain why we should love the best, but will never explain why we should love the moron.

A dead body can float downstream: it can go with the current: it can "be in the swim." To resist the current, even the current of popular opinion, is the property of a live body.

There is one system of morals that has been resisting the current of the way men live for centuries, a system which believes that every man is a shining silver arrow shot out from the bow of this world to the mark of eternal happiness. There are other moral systems that float downstream, and the new pre-faces to morals are of this kind. The "new morality" of May will be the "antiquated morality" of June. Then a new carcass will be thrown into the stream, and as it floats the vultures of the air will feed upon it as their food for the month, and when night shall have passed away and the sun shall have risen over the eastern hills, Christ will be seen walking on the waters.

LOYALTIES GONE ASTRAY

LOYALTIES GONE ASTRAY

I WONDER what would be the general feeling of Americans if they picked up the morning paper to read a bold and startling article by a general of the United States Army entitled: "The Unreasonableness of Defending America"? The surprise, no doubt, would be proportionate to the defense one would justly expect a great soldier to make of a great country. Something of that surprise and wonder comes over me when I read articles by otherwise well-informed and distinguished clergymen, attacking the very cause they are supposed to defend. When a man puts on the garment of a chemist, we expect him to defend the science of chemistry, and when a man puts on the robes of a prophet we expect him to be prophetic. But how often it happens that those who are charged with the defense of the supernatural are those who claim that it is only natural. It is always sad to see loyalties go astray, but particularly the very loyalties of God.

The following passage is typical of the naturalistic attack on the part of those who are supposed to be "divines," but who unfortunately are the most human of humans. "Of course, what all humanists desire to escape is supernaturalism, but in this they have the cordial agreement of a great body of theists. Supernaturalism is an obsolete word and it stands for an obsolete idea. Its history displays its irrelevancy to modern thought. Starting with a whimsical world, where everything that occurred was the direct volition of a human or an extra-human agent, mankind has laboriously discovered a natural world, observed its regularities, plotted its laws, and as one area after another has thus been naturalized, the supernatural inevitably has shrunk. It has become the limbo of the as yet inexplicable, a concept with which we cover our ignorance. The partition of our world into a natural world overlaid by a supernatural order which keeps breaking through, is to a well-instructed mind impossible."

This statement, typical of a dozen others like it, fairly bristles with half-truths, and after all, a half-truth, like a half-cocked gun, is far more dangerous than a lie. It might be interesting to subject three of these half-truths to a critical analysis.

1. The history of the supernatural does not "display its irrelevancy to modern thought." If there is one idol that modern thought loves to adore, it is the idol of progress. Now progress means an advance not in complexity, but in perfection; or better still, progress means the diminution of the traces of original sin. The supernatural stands for this very ideal, namely, progress of reason in the direction of faith; progress of nature and creaturehood in the direction of Divine filiation and sainthood; and progress from the despair of naturalism to the glorious liberty of the children of God. Furthermore, if "modern thought" craves for new emergents in the unfolding of the cosmic process, why should it not welcome the emergence of the supernatural? If it believes in satisfying the needs of the human heart, which craves for something more than the natural, why call that satisfaction "unsuited to our times?" The supernatural is not irrelevant to modern thought, but even though it were irrelevant, would that make it unnecessary or

185

even irreverent? Is modern thought the sole judge of what is best and true and beautiful? May not "modern thought" on this subject be mistaken just as the "modern thought" of the nineteenth century was mistaken? It is one thing to be irrelevant to our moods, but quite another thing to be irrelevant to our needs.

2. "The supernatural" is not synonymous with "the inexplicable," nor is it a "concept with which we cover our ignorance." When it is argued that the "supernatural inevitably has shrunk" with the advance of scientific knowledge, one is arguing not against the supernatural, but against something that has not the slightest relation to it, namely, the false conception of Providence introduced into the thinking world by Isaac Newton over two centuries ago. It is unfortunate that outside of the great Catholic tradition and a few so-called Anglo-Catholics, the supernatural has come to mean what Newton said it was and what many modern thinkers believe it to be: just another name for the unscientific.

Philosophers until Newton's day believed that God was not only the Creator of the world but also a kind Providence; that He not only

186

made the world, but guided that which He had made. But Newton thought of God as doing little more than creating the universe, giving it a flick of His thumb, throwing it off into space, and letting it function largely independently. God had only two duties in this universe, according to Newton. His first duty was to prevent the fixed stars from falling to space, and His second duty was to repair the universe when it ran amuck, lest the comets, which run in eccentric orbs, and the planets, which travel in concentric orbs, should meet in too violent an embrace. In other words, God merely had to retain the universe in a status quo, and to mend the great cosmic leaks whenever such plumbing became necessary.

Now if the function of God is merely to take care of the irregularities of the universe that Newton could not account for by his science, it is only natural that just as scientists find laws to cover such irregularities, so they will find reasons for dispensing with Providence. If the supernatural means taking care of that which science cannot grasp, then the advance of science will mean the retreat of the supernatural. If the supernatural means the scientifically inexplicable, then the Deists were right, and a man is right in saying that as science "discovered a natural world, observed its regularities, . . . the supernatural inevitably has shrunk" and there is less need for an appeal to an "extra-human agent." But the supernatural means none of these things; it is not grounded on the scientifically inexplicable, but on the rationally explicable; it is not a "concept with which we cover our ignorance," but rather an enlightenment with which we dissipate our ignorance; it is not an "obsolete word"—it is the false idea of it that is obsolete. What the statement given above is attacking is not the supernatural, but that which its author believes to be the supernatural, which is a horse of a different color.

This instance is typical of a thousand others, in which intelligent men of our times, otherwise well informed, begin with some absurd definition of Catholic doctrine and then proceed to reject the doctrine because of its absurdity. A straw man is built up and then burned in effigy, because he is only straw. There is no desire on the part of those who deceive really to deceive, but the sad fact remains that those who have the public ear and are being accepted as major prophets are really very ignorant about some of the fundamental tenets of Christianity. Any one is grossly misinformed concerning the supernatural when he identifies it with the Newtonian misconception of it. For the truth of our statement we refer to the learned work of Professor Edwin A. Burtt, entitled "The Metaphysical Foundations of Modern Physical Sciences," in which he states that the Newtonian confusion of the supernatural with the unexplained "proved a veritable boomerang to his cherished philosophy of religion. Really the notion of the Divine eye as constantly roaming the universe on the search for leaks to mend, or gears to replace in the mighty machinery, would have been quite laughable, had not its pitifulness become evident earlier. For to stake the present existence and activity of God on imperfections in the cosmic engine was to court rapid disaster for theology. In short, Newton's cherished theology was rapidly peeled off by all competent hands that could get at him, and the rest of his metaphysical entities and assumptions, shorn of their religious setting, were left to

189

wander naked and unabashed through the premises of subsequent thought, unchallenged by thorough criticism because supposed as eternally based on the positive scientific conquests of the man who first annexed the boundless firmament to the domain of mathematical mechanics." Many a missile has been aimed at the supernatural, but it has struck the wrong target, namely, Newton. But what is not quite so fortunate is that the great mass of hungry hearts in our country who read such attacks on the supernatural as the one above will think that it has slain a dragon, when really it has almost slain God.

3. The relation between the order of nature and grace is not that of a "natural world overlaid by a supernatural order which keeps breaking through." The supernatural order is not related to the natural order as frosting is to a cake, or as the sunlight is shining through a tiny hole in an igloo; the supernatural is related to the natural order vitally and organically, as fruit is to a tree, or knowledge to study. The supernatural is not necessarily the miraculous production of natural effects, or the mechanism of the First Cause acting to the exclu-

sion of the will; rather, it is the ensemble of effects that exceed the nature and power of the natural order, which effects are gratuitously produced by God for the purpose of raising man above his native sphere to a God-like life and destiny.

In the broad sense of the term, the supernatural pervades all creation. Plant life, for example, is "supernatural" in relation to chemical life, for the plant has activities and processes that chemicals have not; animal life is "supernatural" in relation to plant life, for animal life has sensitive and locomotive power that plant life has not; finally, human life is "supernatural" in relation to animal life, for man has an intelligence and free will, which animals have not. Suppose, now, that marble suddenly bloomed and gave forth sweet scents of perfume; would not that be a "supernatural" act for marble? Suppose a flower suddenly became endowed with five senses and moved about with the grace of a swan from shade to sunlight; would not that be a "supernatural" act for a flower? Suppose that a dog suddenly became conscious like a man, put off his bark, and put on speech, quoted Shakspere like an actor, and uttered syllogisms like an Aristotle; would not these be "supernatural" acts for an animal?

These would be supernatural acts in a certain sense, inasmuch as blooming does surpass the nature of marble, and speech the nature of a dog, but such things might possibly have taken place if God had willed to empower original matter so to evolve one into the other. But when we come to man, the supernatural in the strictest sense comes into play. Man by nature is a creature—a product of the hand of the Divine Artist—related to God in the same way as a statue is related to the sculptor. By a free act, Almighty God has willed to make man more than man, namely, His own adopted son, a member of the family of the Trinity and an heir of Heaven. But to become a child of God, and be born of God, belongs far less to the nature of man as man than blooming belongs to the nature of marble. In fact, it surpasses the exigencies and rights of man far more than becoming a living, palpitating member of the sculptor's family belongs to the statue he has chiseled in his studio. Man by nature can call God "Lord," but only by the

192

elevation to a new order can he call God "Father."

But if the supernatural is a gift, is it an "intrusion," as it has sometimes been called? It was an "intrusion" for Luther, who said that the supernatural was like a cloak about one's shoulders, but this was a distorted notion of its true meaning. The supernatural never intrudes on the natural. It is the perfection of the natural; it perfects it much in the same way as bearing fruit is the perfection of the tree. God does not work from the outside of man, but from the inside. He does not so much descend as an intruder as He elevates as a Benefactor. The process is biological throughout. Plants are transformed into man when they enter into our organism as food; man does not intrude on plant life. Rather, he elevates plant life, making it so much a part of him that in him plants take on a new life, a new being, new activities. So too, when man is reborn in Christ by dying to himself in Baptism, he is transformed, not substantially of course, but transformed in his faculties, so that he thinks the thoughts of God, wills the will of God, enjoys the affection of God, and all this to a point where he can

193

cry out, "I live, no, not I, but Christ liveth in me."

Certainly no one would say that God "intruded" on the human nature of Jesus, when God assumed it in personal union with His very Godhead. Why then say that the continuation of the Incarnational process is an intrusion? Cannot God still unite Himself with men according to the pattern of the Incarnation? Can He not perfect the human intelligence by faith, and human energy by grace, and if He does so, thus elevating the son of man to a very adopted Son of God, is not that a progress in the direction of life, truth, and beauty? The modern man who has lost his faith, lost his way, and thrown away the address of his true home, is suffering from the burden of carrying his own nature without the help of supernature. To ask man to be natural is asking man to be unnatural; to call the supernatural the "obsolete" is to rob men of their birthright.

Man has always wanted to be like God and man has always been right in wanting that likeness. He was wrong only when some one on a tree told him that to be like God was to be independent of God; he was right when Some

One else on the Tree of the Cross told him that to be like God was to be dependent on Him like a son. This is the supernatural; and when I hear men with loyalties to Christ decry the supernatural, I feel as if they were trying to sap the blood of the King of Kings from our veins and make us not gods, but just men.

THE SOUL AND THE TWITCHINGS OF
BEHAVIORISM

THE SOUL AND THE TWITCHINGS OF BEHAVIORISM

MAN is a machine and the Behaviorists are his prophets. The fad in psychology called Behaviorism has produced something flattering to our machine age; by extravagantly praising movement, by "emphasizing what man is doing," by asserting that man is just a series of twitchings, muscle-squirmings, visceral reactions, and gland-oozings, by stressing the fact that human activities are due to "something going on in the guts and the glands," Behaviorism is supposed to have done away with the necessity of appealing to a soul or a vital principle in man. In a word, the Behaviorists make psychology a study of the psychological reactions of the organism as a whole; they analyze human nature, not with the eighteenth century, into sensations and ideas, but rather into the completely biological reaction of the nervous system to specific stimuli.

Apart from the fact that Behaviorism has received a severe criticism on the part of the

Gestalt psychologists of Germany, there seem to be other very fundamental criticisms to be urged against a psychology which says that man is made up only of muscle-jerkings, stimuli, and responses. These criticisms contend that the Behavioristic explanation of life is insufficient, because it cannot account for three things: first, bright ideas; secondly, a sense of humor; and thirdly, nonsense.

It is quite true that when the human eye is stimulated by a light, it sees, and when the ear is stimulated by sound, it hears. But it does not follow from this that man is only a machine made up of actions and reactions, like the piston of a cylinder or the behavior of an animal. The eye, though it is adapted for vision, can suffer a twofold harm by a too powerful stimulus such as an ultra-violet light. A very bright light will not only impair the vision, but it will also make the eye inapt for seeing other things. The ear, though adapted to sound, if it is stimulated by an excessive sound such as an explosion will become temporarily deaf and thus make it unable to hear other sounds. In other words, where the stimulus is too powerful, the power of sensation is killed.

Now if the nature of man as an intelligent being is the same as the nature of an animal, why is it that when a Behaviorist has a bright idea, the bright idea does not follow the law that applies to bright lights? Why does not a bright idea, like the idea of "God," or of "justice," destroy the intellect as a bright light destroys the eye? Why does it not impair the intellect for further thinking, as a bright light impairs the eye for further vision? If man is only an animal, and thinking is no different from animal behavior, then the same law should apply to bright lights and bright ideas. But as a matter of fact the same law does not apply. On the contrary, a bright idea, like the idea of "God," not only does not befog and benumb the mental faculties, but gives them greater clarity for the understanding of the universe and the problems of life, for in the light of that idea a thousand other things become clear.

Furthermore, if intellectual activity were merely a question of nerve-centers and organic reactions, then fatigue should increase in direct ratio with the sublimity and intensity of the intellectual vision, just as the senses become fatigued if they are too strongly excited. The contrary, however, is the case; the contemplation of sublime truths, instead of fatiguing the intellect and putting it in a state of incapacity for further thought, excites it and equips it for further ascensions and excursions into the realm of the spiritual. Certainly, if thought were just a matter of sensible reactions, then it should follow the law of all sensible reactions. But the very fact that it does not follow these, leads me to believe that there is something non-material, non-glandular, and non-corporeal, which we call the soul. A man can go blind looking at the sun, but no man even went intellectually blind looking to the Sun of Justice. This can only be because the eye of the mind is different in nature from the eye of the body, and any psychologist who attempts to reduce one to the other is on bad intellectual behavior, regardless of how much he insists on labeling himself a Behaviorist.

Another thing that Behaviorism cannot account for is a sense of humor and its delightful aftermath, laughter. Laughter is caused by seeing the unexpected relations between two judgments, and since a relation can be perceived only by something spiritual, it follows that only a man with a spiritual principle can laugh. Take, for example, this story. A visitor once said to a little girl of six, "What will you do, my dear child, when you are as big as your mother?" "Diet," answered the child. Now that is not a particularly good story, I admit, but assuming that you have been charitable enough to laugh at it, let me use it to prove my point. There are in that story twenty-nine words. Now suppose a dog, a cat, or a canary was in the room at the same time the child made that answer. The dog and the cat and the canary would have received exactly the same auditory stimuli. They would have heard the sounds produced by twenty-nine words. Now, why is it that the dog, the cat, or the canary did not smile at hearing those words, whereas the visitor who asked the child smiled, though perhaps it did very much embarrass the child's mother? It is because the visitor out of those twenty-nine words got thirty reactions. In other words, *he got something out of them that was not in them.* The visitor had to see a double meaning in the word "big," namely, the age meaning and the size meaning.

But in order to see both meanings at one and the same time, which is the condition of understanding any pun, one must not only be material but also spiritual. If a box is filled with salt, it cannot be filled with pepper at one and the same time. And if the mind is filled only with matter, namely, the auditory sensation of "big," it cannot see the word "big" in the other sense that produces laughter.

That is where all Behavioristic and mechanistic explanations of life fail. They cannot account for that wonderful madness called laughter. Nothing in lower creation ever produced anything even remotely resembling a laugh. There is no such thing as some animals beginning to smile and then man breaking out into a laugh. There is something absolutely new when we come to man. The pony did not give a smile and the truck-horse, a horse-laugh. The early hyenas did not merely grin and the later ones laugh—they only have their mouths open. The small valleys did not begin to titter and the bigger ones rock with laughter. One never meets a smile until one comes to man, and the only reason one meets it in man is because man has a soul that can rise above matter and see the relations between things, and in particular the funny ones that help to make life more amusing. There is more truth than mere poetry in saying that man "breaks" out into a laugh, for it is a positive break away from everything below him in creation. It is a break with the past, it is a break with matter, it is the beginning of spirit.

The third defect of Behaviorism is its inability to account for nonsense, and in a day when the screeching of owls is taken for wisdom, the world certainly needs a philosophy that will account for nonsense. Behaviorism holds that man is nothing more than the complexes of "receptors," "conductors," and "effectors"; and that conditioned by the same stimuli he will always react in identically the same way. In this sense man is a machine. Now we never attribute nonsense to a machine, except by exaggeration. If, for example, key 7 and key 6 of an adding-machine are stimulated and they respond with the total of 57, we do not say that the machine is "crazy," or that it has done a "nonsensical" thing. We simply say that it has "gone wrong." But if a man adds 7 and 6 so as to make 57, we say that he is guilty of mathematical nonsense. Mr. Dumb was once asked by a dandruff-remedy company for a testimonial, and he responded: "Before using your dandruff remedy I had two bald spots. Now I have only one." That statement is colossal nonsense of which no machine is capable. Now if man is only a machine, and the sum of nerve-reactions, why do we attribute nonsense only to man and not to a machine; if there is no essential difference between man and an adding-machine, except that man's machinery is slightly damper, how account for the nonsense in the case of man, and the attribution merely of efficiency in the case of a machine? It can only be because a machine is mechanical and determined, and therefore *must* do certain things, whereas man is spiritual, free, and therefore *ought* to do certain things. It is the difference between the "must" of machinery and the "ought" of man that makes nonsense possible. "Ought" immediately takes us out of the realms of machinery and physiology.

As Professor Eddington has so well put it, "Starting with æther, electrons, and other physical machinery, we cannot reach conscious man and render count of what is apprehended in his consciousness. Conceivably, we might reach a human machine interacting by reflexes with its environment; but we cannot reach rational man morally responsible to pursue the truth as to æther, electrons, or religion. . . . In a world of æther and electrons we might perhaps encounter nonsense; we can never encounter damn nonsense."

After all, it is a small thing in life to account for the twitchings, twistings, and squirmings of baby life. Commerce, social life, philosophy, peace conferences, education, and religion—all of these could go on without the slightest advertence to a system of psychology that reduces personality to "a reaction mass as a whole," for the whole world knows, in its moments of sanity, that no matter how many jumping Mexican beans were put into a bag and shaken together, the sum of their "reaction-mass as a whole" would never make them become conscious of themselves.

The world could get along without that kind of psychology, but it could never get along without bright ideas, a sense of humor, and an explanation for the nonsense of Behaviorism.

Behaviorism fails to account for these three things, and it is better to scrap Behaviorism than to run the risk of losing our sense of humor. It is not often that we can quote the Hon. Bertrand Russell with approval, but he spoke words of wisdom when he said, "Modern psychology consists of the discovery by professors of what everybody else has already known," and one of the things that everybody has already known is that, over and above the muscle-twitchings of every human organism, there is a something that twitches which is not psychological, nor biological, but spiritual, and that is the twitching of a conscience.

Mechanistic interpretations of life, such as Behaviorism, are becoming a thing of the past. The distinguished physiologist, James S. Haldane, has said that "the mechanistic speculations of the last century no longer afford any prospect of understanding life." This is the first step toward a return to the psychology of the soul. Psychology first lost its soul, then it lost its mind, finally it lost its consciousness. Driven from bad to worse, and from worse to Behaviorism, it was bound to suffer a reaction. This reaction is now manifested by those scientists who assert that mechanism does not explain life nor thought.

Some one once told the story of a man who went out from England in a row-boat, came back, and made a great discovery—he discovered England. It is not unlikely that in the near future, the psychologists who left the shores of sane thinking in the row-boat *Novelty* will soon come back to those shores once again, and will make a great discovery—they will discover a soul. And those who make that discovery will be hailed as original thinkers, for if error multiplies, the most novel and original thing in the world will be truth.

THE NEW PELAGIANISM

MODERN paganism is doing the same thing the Christian world has always done, but is doing it for a different reason. It has retained the external form of things but emptied their content and meaning. Christian terms and practices are retained, consecrated words of revealed religion are used—but they are retained and used in the same fashion that a new firm trades under the old name, in order to win the goodwill of its former customers. The Christian world, for example, recommends fasting; the modern world fasts, too, under the name of "dieting," not to make the soul beautiful, but rather to make the body beautiful. The Christian world recommends examination of conscience: the modern world does the same, under the guise of psychoanalysis. The Christian world recommends telling one's sins to a confessor: the pagan world recommends telling them to the world. In the first instance, however, the reason for the confession is to elevate the soul by purification: in the second, it is to ease the body by sublimation. Another example of this tendency is furnished us by our movie world. Hollywood is fascinated by the Cross of Christ, just as Christians are, but not because the Cross is the prelude to the empty tomb, but rather because it is the prelude to a full purse: it is good business.

The world thus becomes blighted not only by bad things but also by good things; a patronage is shown towards the better things of life that at times becomes more intolerable than persecution. In this connection, Mr. Chesterton has written: "By its own radical incapacity for restraint or dignity or honorable privacy, it is spoiling all the good things as instruments of good. The virtues it is too weak to practise it is sufficiently strong to weaken. All that is hard in fact it will make soft with fiction: and make a cant even of death and pain and the last reserves of humanity."

In keeping with this general attitude to do Christian things for an unchristian reason, is to be noted a very old movement that is thought to be very new, namely, Humanism. Humanism has been defined as "the endeavor to keep the best spiritual values of religion while surrendering any theological interpretation of the universe." In its broadest sense it is an endeavor to have Christianity without Christ, godliness without God, and Christian hope without the promise of another life.

This description of it is fairly accurate, but it does not describe it in all its phases. Humanism, like many other "isms," suffers from want of definiteness. There are some of its minor prophets who make it little better than a vague humanitarianism. Others, on a slightly higher level, like Polonius, by many "indirections find directions out" and end by making any old test-tube a refuge to preserve us from being eaten away by "the acids of modernity." Then there is the more classical type, whose Humanism sees the fallacy behind the sentimental gush of the philosophy of religious experience that has its source in Rousseau, and the pragmatic-scientific glorification of the forces of nature, which has its source in Francis Bacon. It has even dared to be called "unmodern" by challenging the fallacies of a religion that is nothing more than a sociology, a morality that is nothing but new scientific names to excuse old sins, and an ethics that is the line of least resistance parading under the false colors of "self-expression." More than that, it has sought to make leisure meaningful by filling it up with contemplation and silence, and to make the conflict of passions in man intelligible in the light of the dualism of spirit and matter.

There is something common to these three forms of Humanism, and what is common is something very old—in fact, fifteen hundred years old. That old common factor is Pelagianism. That is why we have entitled this chapter on Humanism, "The New Pelagianism."

It is curious and interesting that Pelgianism and Humanism both began with men who knew their Plato and their Stoics better than their Christianity. Both were started by men of the West influenced by Eastern ideas; both movements have emphasized the will at the expense of the intellect and grace. The difference between the two movements is in their environment. Pelagianism appeared in a society in which there was great intellectual light, and hence its shortcomings very soon became apparent. Humanism, on the contrary, appears in

216

a society in which most of the lights have gone out, and hence appears wiser than it really is, for a lantern in darkness is more satisfying than a lantern in the sunlight.

What was Pelagianism? It was a doctrine taught by a great student of Greek philosophy, Pelagius by name, who held that human nature by its own power is able to save itself without the help of God's grace. This is the central doctrine of Humanism. Note the parallel between the two. Both deny original sin, but both admit the conflict of matter and spirit as a psychological factor; both deny that it is necessary to have recourse to the grace of Christ, though admitting the beauty of Christ; finally, both appeal to the will of man as sufficient to save without the new motive force of grace, which makes man a child of God rather than a creature.

The old Humanism under the name of Pelagianism was finally condemned at the Council of Carthage in May, 418. A new Humanistic movement soon followed in its wake. The Semi-Pelagians, made up of monks of Marseilles, admitted, in response to the decrees of Carthage, that man needs grace, but held that by natural good works man could merit grace. The Semi-Pelagians thus made concessions to the supernatural that the Pelagians did not make, just as some of our present-day Humanists make concessions to the supernatural that others do not make. In its essence, the Humanism of to-day is nothing but a revival of Pelagianism; it is the heresy of human action and intellection, the assertion that humanity can climb divine heights without divine help, and that of itself and by itself it is sufficient for the perfection of its capacities and powers. Briefly, it is the assertion that the human mind needs not faith and human power needs not grace.

Humanism has the two fatal defects of Pelagianism: first, it fails to take account of the great failure of Humanism in the past, and secondly, it is too inhuman.

Humanism fails to take account of the sad lesson humanity had learned during the four thousand years previous to the Incarnation, namely, that neither by his own human knowledge nor by his own human power is man able to make himself a perfect man even in the natural order. The two great peoples that divided the pre-

218

Incarnational world bear witness to this sad truth—the Jews and the Gentiles.

The Gentiles, principally, have proved to all posterior civilizations that man by his own *knowledge* cannot reach Humanistic perfection. The Greeks, masters of philosophy and well skilled in what our modern Humanists call "decorum," fell into the grossest of errors. Plato, for example, otherwise so beautifully human, held that women were the property of soldiers, and Aristotle, though admitting a Supreme First Cause, denied that a Providence rules the spheres. Epicurus founded a school on pleasure, and Zeno built another on the foundations of vanity, one degrading man to the level of a beast, the other exalting him to the heights of intoxicated pride. Pythagoras taught that man was the measure of all things, as do our own Pragmatists to-day; Pyrrhus led men to believe that there was no such thing as certainty, just as modern skeptics assure us that they are certain there can be no such thing as certainty.

Not only in the age of Pericles, but in the age of Augustus—not only in the land of Greeks, but in that of the Romans as well—

human minds were testifying to the need of another light besides that of reason. In the practical moral order, the wife was the slave of passion; children were exposed at the city gates to be devoured by wolves. A slave was crucified because he broke a vase. Even the hands that signed the condemnation of others now turned against themselves, and tearing out their own hearts, perished with the forlorn cry of hopeless hell, "Virtue, thou art only a name!" Lucretius explains away the gods as myths; Cicero tells us that in his day philosophy and atheism were synonymous; Seneca denied that there is anything beyond the graces; Horace, as hard as a Pharisee, does not hesitate to say that death is too good for an impure vestal, but at the same time urges us to "seize pleasure while it flies, for 'tis of heaven the gift"; a merchant kneels before Mercury and prays that he may cheat his customers; and a lawyer before his favorite goddess begs that a cloak of virtue may cover his deceits and frauds.

The very light of reason was going out. Men began by transferring the cult of God to their intellectual genii. Then they began to see gods in the air and the earth, in fire and water. Deification of nature followed, and the sun and moon and stars were worshiped as deities. Finally, a last plunge, God became simply a divinized man, and idolatry the rule. Profound forgetfulness of God, and an unutterable contempt of man—the two are inseparable, one always engendering the other. Amidst such abused knowledge of both the speculative and the moral order, Tertullian could say with some truth to the Roman magistrates, "Who is there among you who can say he has not put his own child to death?"

If the Gentile bore witness to the inability of human *knowledge* to satisfy the demands of perfect Humanism, it is the Jew who has witnessed to the inability of human *power* to produce a perfect human being without divine grace. From the time of Adam until Moses, those who were destined to become the chosen people learned the same lesson as the Gentiles —the insufficiency of pure Humanistic wisdom. Then God gave them knowledge, a knowledge not like that of the nations, but a higher kind descending from Heaven. From out the thunder and lightning of Sinai, when mountain rocked and people feared, God gave to

221

Moses and his people a new knowledge, a higher code of morality—the knowledge of the Law, the Ten Commandments. In so many words God was saying to them: "Your own human wisdom is insufficient. Now I shall give you knowledge." It remained to be seen whether with their knowledge they had the power and the will to put it into practice.

But alas, even while Moses was receiving the law, his people rose up against his brother, saying: "Make us gods that will go before us." The commandments of God are forgotten. Core, Dathan, and Abiron deny the special prerogatives of the priesthood of Aaron and the divine mission of Moses and assert a lay priesthood without divine call or unction. David, later on, rich with the spoils of the world, and wanting nothing for his material happiness, falls into adultery and then is guilty of the murder of Urias, with whose wife he has committed his shameful sin. Of the twenty kings who ruled over Judea, the greater number disgracefully served idols; two of them even offered their own children in sacrifice to Moloch; Acahaz closed the temple to worshipers and Manasses

222

set up altars to the false gods in the outer courts.

Even with the knowledge of what was right and wrong, they became "transgressors from their wombs," seeking "comfort in idols under every green tree and sacrificing children in torrents." With desolation was the whole land made desolate, because there was no one who considered in his own heart.

Forty centuries of Humanistic experiment had passed, and humanity had learned the lesson of the insufficiency of human knowledge and human power. Help was needed; Humanism was not enough. Cries multiplied to God, not only on the part of the Jews, who asked for the heavens to bud down a Saviour, but also on the part of the Greeks, who in their great tragedies pleaded for a Redeemer in the words of Æschylus:

> Do not look
> For any end moreover to this curse
> Ere some god appear to accept thy pangs
> On his own head vicarious.

In answer to the yearnings of Humanist hearts, there appeared from out the heavens

223

Christ the Son of God, "the Power and the Wisdom of God"—the Power the Jews were seeking, and the Knowledge the Gentiles were craving.

But some insisted that Humanism was enough, and of these it has been written: "He came unto His own and His own received Him not." To the Jews He was a "stumbling-block," because Power came in the weakness of the Cross; to the Gentiles, He was "foolishness," because Knowledge came in the form of one Who "never learned," and yet taught a wisdom that was folly to the world. "But unto them that are called, both Jews and Greeks, Christ is the Power of God and the Wisdom of God —for the foolishness of God is wiser than men and the weakness of God is stronger than men."

Our modern Humanists who ask us to reject the superhuman Christ, either because eternal life is not necessary or because faith in Him is reducible to "imagination," are asking us to fly in the face of forty centuries of experiment. They would have us relive the world-experiment that ended in the Incarnation and believe that man should try once more to carry on with the sufficiency of human power without grace, and act as if the God becoming man means nothing to man. To ask us to do this is to commit the typical sin of Occidental civilization, the sin of pride.

The Oriental world fell into the excess of believing that God does everything and man does nothing—that is, Oriental mysticism and quietism. Our Occidental world has fallen into the other excess of believing that man does everything and God does nothing—this is Humanism. The true position is the mean: Man can do something with the help of God's sustaining grace. The Oriental world needs to learn from Paul: "I can do all things in Him Who strengtheneth me," and the Occidental Humanists need to learn the words of our Blessed Lord Himself: "Without Me you can do nothing."

This brings us to the second criticism of Humanism; it is too inhuman—it places too great a burden on poor human nature. Human nature in virtue of an immortal soul has something infinite about it; it has infinite aspirations and craving for truth, beauty, love, and life; it refuses to be pacified by the pleasures of time and space, ever anxious, as it were, to "swing the world a trinket at one's wrist," and mount on to the "hid battlements of Eternity," where there is nothing but the Infinite Perfection of the Life of God. The Humanist will admit the infinity of these aspirations, and therein lies the fallacy. To ask man to satisfy this passive capacity for the infinite by an appeal to the finite; to drink the waters of time to slake the thirst for eternity; to feed on corruptible food to satisfy the hunger for the Everlasting Bread of Life, and to rest in the human when one craves for the divine—this is to hamper human nature in all that makes it human. This is not human, though one does call it Humanism.

It is a strange paradox, but a true one, nevertheless, that man only becomes most human when he becomes most divine, because he has been destined from all eternity to be conformable to the image of the Son of God. Any form of Humanism, therefore, which denies the necessity of grace, and attempts to perfect man without it, is asking man to grow without an environment in which to grow. To remain on the level of the purely human, and to hold up the ideal of "decorum," is to permit man to expand horizontally, in the direction of the human, but not vertically, in the direction of the divine. Humanism allows for the spreading out of man on the plane of nature, but not for his being lifted up on the plane of grace, and elevation is far more important than expansion. Deny the order of grace, the realm of the Fatherhood of God, and what environment has humanity to grow in except poor weak humanity like himself? Plants live thanks to an environment outside themselves, an environment with which their structure is in harmony. Since the soul is spiritual, man needs the environment not only of humanity, which belongs to the realm of his body, but that of spirit, which belong to his soul, and it is only by entering into harmony with that great environment that he attains the end of his creation. That is why Humanism without the superhuman is not Humanism but Naturalism. Man by nature is not an idol but an idolator, and to turn back upon himself is to condemn him to selfishness, which is death.

Humanism, denying the absolute necessity of Christ, suffers from the fatal defect of all such denials: It asks man to worship a system, and that, too, is inhuman. Humanism as a philosophical system is flattering indeed to the intellectual élite, but offers little consolation to the man without a job or to a heart burdened with sin. Not every one can be cultured. There were simple shepherds as well as wise men at the crib of Christ, and no one will deny that they had a place there. Love of the best is an easy ideal to follow when those whom we love are the best, but it means little when we are face to face with those who, from the human point of view, are not worth loving, such as the broken human earthenware of our big city streets who carry sandwich signs to inform the rich of new luxuries. There is only one reason for loving those who are not worth loving, and that is because Some One loved us—we who are not worth loving.

We have too many systems to-day, and that is why the hearts of men have grown cold. Systems are too abstract. "Decorum," "common decency," and the like do well on paper, but unless "decorum," "love," "charity," become incarnate, man will never respond. Systems of love mean nothing, but make that love appear in a person and it means something. So, too, let "decorum," "restraint," "sacrifice," appear in the person of God Incarnate and men will respond. That is why Mr. Chesterton, in speaking of the response to the person of Christ in Catholicism, could so aptly say: "There are three hundred million people in the world who accept the mysteries that I accept and live by the faith I hold. I really want to know whether it is anticipated that there will be three hundred million Humanists in humanity."

There is the difference between the Church and Humanism. The Church appeals to a person, Humanists to a philosophy. The Church says Humanism consists in reflecting in our own lives the eternal image of the person of Christ; Humanists say Humanism consists in reflecting in our lives the abstractions of Oriental mysticism or those of Stoic philosophy.

Humanism, then, is good as far as it goes, but it does not go far enough. It forgets that life is not only a push from below but also a gift from above, and that man in his noble Humanistic strivings has been met half-way on the upward road by the Person of Christ, Who came to earth to take not merely the hand of man, but his very nature, to divinize it, to lift it up into intimacy with God, so as to call God "Father," and to make of it the source and pattern of a continued Incarnation, in which we would become better men because other Christs.

This is the true Humanism in which we can call one another "brother" because we have learned to call God "Father," and we cannot call God "Father" unless He has a "Son." No! Man cannot save himself, if it was God who first saved him. In the language of Augustine, "But if God has saved him, then what will man be, for whom God became man!" To think this out is to think out the death of Humanism.

THE PHILOSOPHY OF CHARITY

THE PHILOSOPHY OF CHARITY

THERE is a philosophy behind charity as there is a philosophy behind everything else in life. It is that philosophy in relation to the tendencies in modern social service which this chapter seeks to discover and analyze in the light of Catholic philosophy.

The first tendency in modern charity, if we are correctly observing contemporary movement, is towards greater organization, even to the extent of making it one of the big business concerns of the country. The bread-basket stage, the penny-in-a-tin-cup stage, the hand-out stage, have given way to the bureau and the scientific-giving stage. Statistics are replacing sympathy, and social workers are replacing emotions. The complexities of modern life, the crisscrossing of economic and personal factors, demand a discipline in giving, and a skill in investigation, that can be attained only by the organized effort of those specially trained in such work and thoroughly conversant with such conditions. Whether or not this tendency is a desirable one is at present not the point at issue. It is the facts we are seeking, and to elaborate further the obviousness of the tendency towards organization would be only gilding the lily.

The second tendency in modern charity is towards a deification of society at the expense of the individual. The philosophical principle behind this tendency is not that of the common good, which claims that individuals shall effectively coöperate for the well-being of society, but rather the principle that individuals should be submerged for the sake of the collectivity. In a text well known to social workers, one finds such a philosophy in these words, "Human nature itself is now regarded as a product of social intercourse"—which statement implies that society creates human nature, rather than that human nature creates society. Of the same mind, another sociologist carries glorification of society to the detriment of the individual to such a height that he makes "the service of God consist in the service of men," and consequently denies any such thing as an indi-

234

vidual sin. The only sin is the social sin; "disloyalty to society."

The final tendency in modern philanthrophy is towards absoluteness—not in the sense that it seeks to rid the world of poverty, crime, and disease, but in the sense that the alleviation or partial elimination of these ills constitutes its full and final purpose. Giving bread means filling empty stomachs—it means nothing more and it can mean nothing more. Improving home conditions means better sunlight, better food, warmer temperature—and nothing more. There is no other purposiveness behind social work than the tangible, and no other finality than the eradication from society of the "d's" —dependents, defectives, and delinquents. Any vision beyond that which can be embraced in a budget or compiled statistically or touched by hands is regarded as a form of idealism to which these philanthropists feel a positive antipathy. It is assumed throughout the whole process of alleviating the ills of mankind that mankind has no other destiny than the present, and that the fruits of helpfulness and philanthropy, if they extend beyond a stomach, a

235

playground, or a clinic, never go any further than a formula gleaned from those experiences.

If our finger has been properly kept on the pulse of modern philanthropy, it would seem to indicate a triple condition or tendency: (1) A tendency towards organization as regards its *form;* (2) A tendency towards the hypersocial at the expense of the individual as regards its *method;* (3) A tendency towards the absolute as regards its *purpose.*

Now, what interpretation does the traditional philosophy of charity bring to these tendencies? Does it disapprove them, does it approve them, or does it inject a new spirit into them and consequently transform them? Catholic thought is essentially a transforming thought, elevating the baser things to higher planes in the hierarchy of values, thanks to its power of divine alchemy.

The true philosophy of charity would not condemn these modern tendencies and ask for their destruction. Rather, it would ask that they be elevated to conform to these three principles:

(1) Charity must not only be organized, but must also be organic; (2) Charity must

deal not only with society but also with individual souls; (3) Charity must not be absolute, but sacramental, i. e., not only of the earth earthy but of the heavens heavenly.

The assumption behind organized charity is that charity work becomes organized when individuals come together and unite themselves for the purpose of remedying the social ills of mankind, as men might come together and form a club. It is further assumed that charity work develops horizontally, that is, it begins with men and ends with men, proceeding from the organization through the social worker and finally out to the needy. There is thought to be no difference in kind, but only one of degree, between the will of the man, which calls the organization into being, and the poor disorganized men who receive the fruits of the organization.

This conception of charity is not the Christlike one. For us, the source of charity is not the will of men, but the will of God. The origin of charity lies not in effective human groupings but in divine life, and hence its development or unfolding is not horizontal, like the history of a human institution, which begins with men

237

and ends with men, but vertical, beginning with God at its summit, and ending with man as its term. According to our philosophy, charity begins within the bosom of the Triune God, for charity is the definition of God. From out that infinite source, charity comes in a never-ending procession, reaching down to our own days. Because charity is naturally expansive and enthusiastic, God by a free act willed that others should share His Love, and so Omnipotence moved and said to nothingness, "Be"; Eternity moved and said to time, "Begin"; Light moved and said to darkness, "Be light" —and lo! living, palpitating things were seen moving among Eden's fourfold rivers. That life rebelled against its God, but charity could not keep the secret of its love, and the telling of the promise of better things was Revelation. God was emptying Himself. He revealed his power in His Creation, His plans in His Revelation, and now last of all, He reveals Himself, and the tiny baby hands that clutched at straws and were not quite long enough to touch the huge heads of the cattle, were the hands of Charity Incarnate—Jesus Christ.

But charity has not exhausted itself. Palestine as a space and three and thirty years as a time were not enough to reveal the richness of that charity. How could they be, since eternity itself is not long enough! And so, He plans to assume another body—not just the physical body that He took from Mary, with which He obeyed her for thirty years, taught for three years, and redeemed for three hours, but a mystical body, made up of all the individual human natures scattered throughout the world —men, women, and children who would be united to Him not by the singing of hymns, by the reading of books, nor merely by following His example, but who would be vitally and organically one with Him by being reborn and regenerated and incorporated into His divine life in such a manner that they would be one with Him, part of Him, sharing His truth, His life, His blood, His love. And that body is His Church. And just as the historical Jesus Christ was true God and true Man—divine and human in the unity of His Divine Person—so too the Church is human in the elements that make it up, divine in its life, and both are one in the unity of Christ. And in this sense, Christ is the Church and the Church is Christ, and hence the voice of one is the voice of the other, and the life of one is the life of the other. The Church then is the mystical body enshrining the charity of Jesus Christ brought to this world in the Incarnation.

Charity, then, is not horizontal, extending from kind-hearted men to needy men, but vertical, extending from the infinite source of charity, God Himself, down to the members of the mystical body, through the Incarnation. Charity, then, is not organized, nor is charity work accomplished through organizations. An organization is an assembly of men for the better securing of a particular object, but there is no intrinsic connection between the controlling head of an organization and its members. Charity is organic, in the sense that it belongs to an organism in which there is a vital connection between the cells or members that make it up, and a vital connection as well between the Head and the body, as in the human organism. Charity may embrace a grouping of men, records, statistics, committees, graphs, and budgets. It may be these, but something more; it is organic—organic because alive with the life of a body; organic because the flesh and

240

blood of its members are the living members of the body of Christ. Looked at from this point of view, the first charity bureau was in Bethlehem, its first case was the case we are still working on—the salvation of humanity through the infinite life of Jesus Christ.

Some very practical conclusions follow from the organic nature of charity. First, the poor, the sick, the unemployed, the orphan, are fellow-members with us in the body of Christ. As St. Paul puts it; "As in one body we have many members but all the members have not the same office; so we, being many, are one body in Christ, and every one members of one another."

Our relations to them are not external, like that of a gardener to his garden, but internal, like the organs of the body. If I burn my finger, my whole body hurts because my finger is inseparable from my whole organism; so too, if there are certain members of Christ's society who are thirsty, hungry, or in need—it is *we*, the whole body, who are thirsty, hungry, and needy, for we are members one of another in the body of Christ. Their needs, their wants, are not theirs but *ours*, and no charity can call

241

itself Christian unless it realizes this. The eye cannot be indifferent to the ear and when it sees a blow directed to the ear, say: "It is not going to strike me. I shall, then, take no pains to avoid it." It does interest the eye, for the eye and ear are parts of the same body, and so the sufferings of the poor weak members of the mystical body are our sufferings, and the sufferings of the body are the sufferings of Christ.

A second conclusion touches on the strictness of our obligation to the poor. There is a charity-sentiment, divine in its inspiration, that we should love all those who are near and dear to us. According to this charity-sentiment, man is in the center of several circumferences. In the first circle is himself; in the second, his family; in the third, his friends; and in the fourth, his nation. The charity-sentiment towards each of these varies in ratio with their distance. As the circumferences widen, affection becomes less, as the heat of the sun becomes less with distance from the source.

But in addition to the charity-sentiment, there is the charity-duty, which is based not only upon natural affection one for another but upon the divine affection of Christ for the members of His body. In the charity-sentiment, it is space or proximity that makes the neighbor; in the charity-duty, it is not proximity, but the love for the increase of the body of Christ, that makes the neighbor. In the charity-duty, not the closest to us, but the farthest away, are our neighbors. Such is the meaning of Paul: "In the charity of Christ, there is neither Greek nor barbarian, Jew nor free"; and the words of Our Divine Lord: "He who loves father or mother, brother or sister, more than Me is not worthy of Me." Who is my neighbor in organic charity? Our Lord answered that question in the parable: It was not the one who was of the same family, the same class, or the same social stratum as those who passed down the road; not the Levite for the Levite, not the priest for the priest, the Samaritan for the Samaritan. The neighbor was one who was not a neighbor—one on the fringe of the circumference of affection, that is, a traveler besieged by robbers. And yet even those in the dim borderland of acquaintance— the chance passer-by on the road, the one whom we have never seen before—all possess a qual-

243

ity that identifies them even with another traveler Who one day sat tired at Jacob's well: "For what you have done to the least of these My brethren, you have done unto *Me*."

The very day that parable was told, organized charity was founded in the words Our Lord put into the mouth of the first social-service worker: "Take care of him and whatsoever thou shalt spend over and above, I, at my return, will repay thee." But it was already *organic*, for how could there be mercy unless there was first justice, and how could there be justice unless Justice Itself had come into the world to set it right with its God?

The second tendency in modern philanthropic work is that of merging the individual into society and regarding society as the unique field of its labors. I believe that there lies behind this tendency a wrong theory of society, inspired for the most part by the school of Lévy-Bruhl and Durkheim, namely, that society is *sui juris* above individuals and independent of them. Their argument runs as follows: A composition is different from the elements that enter into it—for example, water is different from the two atoms of hydrogen and one atom

244

of oxygen. But society is a composition of individuals. Therefore it differs entirely from the individuals that compose it.

This theory of society does not always come to the surface, but it is implied in a thousand and one modern attitudes towards social problems. The sterilization of the unfit, for example, is one form of the philosophy that maintains society's right to mutilate the integrity of human life. Eugenics, too, implies that society has a better right to choose the bride than the bridegroom has; birth-control propagandists and Malthus-minded groups maintain that ushering more children into the world than a society can assimilate is a form of bootlegging and is therefore unethical.

It is our contention that society is not a new being but only a new *mode of being*. Society is made up of like elements, not unlike ones, as the above example would lead us to believe. Adding drops of water to drops of milk does not make water, but milk and water. So, too, adding individual to individual does not constitute a thing separate, distinct, from the individuals but only a new modality of the individuals' existences.

245

Society does not destroy individuals, nor can it exist apart from individuals. It has no unitary consciousness, it being only the resultant of the functional coördination of individuals in an organic whole. And this doctrine of common sense finds further verification in Revelation. The Church or the incarnate charity of Jesus Christ, it has been said, is an organism, a body made up of many members. Now we hasten to add that just as the life of a human organism does not destroy the individual cell-life of its million of cells, so neither does the mystical body of Christ destroy the individuality of the members. We all share the individual life of Christ, and yet there is no absorption, no merging of offices; there still remains diversity of ministries but the same spirit. There is unity but there is also multiplicity.

If society in the natural order, or the mystical body in the supernatural, does not absorb, submerge, or swallow up the individual, it follows that the talk about "social processes," "social prevision," "Humanitarianism," is beside the point. The problems of social work may be stated in the abstract, but *practically*

246

the solution must touch an individual and an individual who has certain inviolable rights.

Juvenile delinquency, for example, is ultimately the problem of the young delinquent; crime is a problem of the criminal; tuberculosis, a problem of the tubercular; poverty, a problem of the poor man or poor woman; flood-relief, a problem neither of the flood nor of relief but of a victim. And so we might go on, always keeping in the back of our heads the sound principle that there is no such thing as humanity; there are only Peters and Pauls, Marys and Anns. And according to Christian doctrine, each of these has an individual soul. Hence social service is dealing not with *something* but *somebody*. Over and over again the Church insists that the least of the individuals, such as the poor human earthenware that is thrown into our gutters and those with focusless eyes who bat their heads against padded cells, is infinitely worth saving because he was infinitely worth redeeming. And any form of philanthropy that forgets the doctrine of the common good for the false principle that society is a new entity for which individuals must be sacrificed, sooner or later will be advocat-

247

ing elimination of the unfit; the murder of defective infants—and then we shall have once more a paganism in which mothers will throw their children from Tarpeian Rocks, and in which new Herods will arise to practise birth-control as he did—even with the sword.

No abstract veneration of society, I care not how idealistic it is, can put a proper worth upon the individual. It is only the Gospel notion of charity, which preaches the individuality of the members of the body of Christ, that can give them dignity. A question naturally proposes itself to our minds: Charity came in with the Incarnation? Will it pass out with the dechristianization of society? What will be the motive force behind helping the poor and the needy fifty years from now if Christ's inspiration passes out of charity? Will love of humanity keep it alive? Hardly, for a self-centered humanity will be just as cold and as chilling as a self-centered individual. As Mr. Chesterton reminds us: "Few people are fired with a direct individual affection for the five people sitting on the other side of a railway-carriage; let us say a wealthy matron, giving to snorting and sneering, a bright little Jew stockbroker, a larger and vacant farmer, a pale and weary youth with a limp cigarette, and a young woman perpetually powdering her nose. All these are sacred beings of equal value in the sight of God with the souls of Hildebrand and Shakespeare; but a man needs to be a little of a mystic to think so." There may be much in humanity that is worth loving, even from human motives, but there is little to love from human motives in the wrecks that come to charities. If there is to be love for them, it must be inspired by Some One Who first loved some one who was not worth loving —I mean Christ loving us—and unless the social worker sees Christ in the needy, he will not long love the needy.

The true philosophy of charity cannot accept without correctives the modern tendency to regard as the absolute end of charity the alleviation of the ills that afflict mankind, nor can it regard as an ideal a society that is free from disease, hospitals and prisons—not because such an ideal is wrong, but because it is incomplete.

It is a tenet of the Catholic philosophy of charity that the lessening of the ills of mankind and the diminution of the traces of disease are not ends in themselves, but rather means to an end. In other words, philanthropy is not absolute in its end but sacramental. In the strict sense of the term, there are seven sacraments— material things used as means of spiritual sanctification. In the broad sense of the term, everything in the world is a sacrament, for everything in the world can be made a means of leading us on to Christ and hastening the reign of Christ.

This world is not a closed, mechanistic, completed achievement; it is rather a scaffolding up which souls climb to the Kingdom of Heaven, and when the last soul shall have climbed up through it, then the scaffolding shall be torn down and burnt with fervent fire, not because it is base, but simply because it has done its work. If this is true of the universe in its entirety, it is true of the littler things in it— bread, money, hospital beds, ministrations of the social worker—for all these are little sacraments, tiny means of spiritual sanctification and nurseries of the Father's eternal mansions. It is only the proximate end of charity that looks to the diminution of social ills. Social ills must be remedied in order that the life of the soul and the spirit may be free to move on to God. It is a very unidealistic social service that ends in filling empty stomachs and empty stockings; it is a Christian social service that fills these things as a prelude to filling empty hearts. One form of charity is the apostolate of truth, and that bureau which has not made its budget show an increase in spiritual harvest for Christ, which has not sacramentalized its work, has fallen just as short of the ideal and end of charity as a certain social worker did who sent his budget to the Lord and it read: "I fast twice in the week, I give tithes of all I possess," etc.

Charity is not absolute; it is sacramental. It is not opaque; it is transparent. The needy members with which we deal are not just needy members: Case No. 365 is not Case No. 365. It is Christ. Even the just social worker will be surprised on the Judgment Day when he learns from Christ: "When you did it to the least of these . . . you did it unto Me."

It is this sacramental, transparent character of charity that lends dignity and worth to its duller and harder side. It is love of society that enables some men to get out from their individual self-centeredness and selfishness. . . . But if there is no Christ beyond society, if there is nothing but society, then where can society find something that will make it forget its self-centeredness and selfishness? We must anchor outside the ship in which we are sailing and the cosmos is too small for even man to do that. If there is any unhappiness in any modern social worker, it must come from his greatness; because there is the infinite in man that with all his cunning he cannot quite bring under the finite.

Charity, in brief, centers about two realities —human natures, who dispense or receive benefices; and things, like gold and silver, clothing and food. Charity embraces in its scope both what we are and what we have.

Since charity involves these two great visibilities of the world, flesh and things, it is fitting that both of them should have figured in the supreme act of charity, which was the Redemption of mankind. And actually both of them did hold a prominent place. First, Christ assumed a human nature—and that was the Incarnation; secondly, He spiritualized material things—and these were the sacraments.

But the Incarnate did not exhaust Himself

in the Incarnation. The Incarnational process continues. Charity workers are therefore to do with these great realities what He did. First of all, we are to offer our individual human natures to Him, that He may continue the work of His Incarnation—human natures with which He might visit the sick, instruct the ignorant, counsel the doubtful, open blind eyes to the light of His sunlight, unstop deaf ears to the music of the human voice. Secondly, we are to make use of things, our possessions, our talents, as kinds of sacraments, each one of which has pronounced over it the consecrating words: "This is offered on account of you, O Lord!" in order that the whole universe may become sacramentalized for His honor and glory.

This is the philosophy of Catholic charity, and since the day charity became organic with us, it has never been quite right to say that God is in His Heaven and all's right with world; for Christ has left the heavens to set it right, and is found amongst us, even as we talk.

COSMICAL RELIGION

COSMICAL RELIGION

PROFESSOR EINSTEIN has offered to the scientific world a hypothesis that at present seems to interpret the facts of the universe better than any other hypothesis. For this he deserves great credit and much praise. When, therefore, a criticism is offered of some of his views I do not wish to be understood as disparaging, in even the slightest way, the achievements of this really distinguished scientist, who in his speculations has ordered a bigger universe than Newton and unified that which even his great predecessor could not unify. What I shall say is in criticism not of a scientist but of a theologian and a philosopher.

Perhaps most of us would be quite satisfied to rest on the laurels of relativity, but not Professor Einstein. Succumbing to the lure of journalists, he has recently stepped out of his field and made pronouncements on education, evolution, and religion.

There is nothing, of course, in the scientific

doctrine of relativity by itself that has any bearing on religion. It is just as indifferent to it as the law of gravitation or the economic law of supply and demand. Relativity of time and space does not mean the relativity of a spatio-temporal religion any more than the imprisoning of ultra-violet rays means an ultra-violet religion. If, therefore, Professor Einstein enunciates a dogma about religion, it is of no more value for religion than the statement of a home-run king about home-brew. There is no more value in the statement of a mathematical physicist turned theologian than there is in the statement of a theologian turned mathematical physicist. If I should gather together a few choice scientific terms like "co-efficient of zero," "gravitational stability," "spatio-temporal continuum," "organic universe of epochal occasions," and weave them into a lecture on mathematical science, I would be doing the absurd and making a fool of myself, for I would have no intellectual warrant for my pronouncements. Now this is precisely what Professor Einstein has done when he pieces together a few ideas of Lucretius and Hume and writes a book on religion. He has

258

no more right to be heard on religion than I have to be heard on mathematics, for the very simple reason that I know nothing about mathematics and he knows nothing about religion.

The reasons why the world accepts him as an authority on religion are weird and curious. It is because he has devised a hypothesis that, it is said, only four men in the world understand. But why should unintelligibility become the reason for the acceptance of a prophet? Christianity asks us to accept its prophet because He rose from the darkness of a grave. The modern world asks us to accept its prophets because they remain in darkness. If Einstein is accepted as an authority because only four men understand his relativity, why should not I be accepted as an authority when I say something that no one in the world can understand—for example, "The occipito-frontalis of the prehensive convolution of the metaphysical disestablishmentarism requires the ordinal numerosity of minus one?" The expression of the unintelligible is no claim to greatness. This is no criticism of Einstein; it is, however, a criticism of those who accept

Einstein on the ground that only four men understand him.

But this is only a surface reflection. In accepting the authority of some one who has expressed that which, for most of us, is unintelligible, the human mind testifies once more to its love of mystery. Einstein is mysterious; that is why the world likes his religion. The human mind likes mystery for the simple reason that it is meant for the mysterious infinite. But here the modern mind falls into a queer inconsistency. On the one hand, it refuses to accept anything beyond reason or without proof and declares that henceforth religion must be free from dogmas and mysteries. On the other hand, it accepts the dogmas of Einstein—every scientific statement is a dogma—and makes a religion out of them because they are mysterious. That brings up the question why the world should accept the mysteries of Einstein rather than the mysteries of Christ.

It will be recalled that when Einstein left the field in which he is one of the world's great masters, and entered the field of religion, he declared that the religion of the future will not be a religion of fear, or of morality, but what he calls a cosmical religion—a religion in which man enters into communion with the great universe round about him.

One of the principal difficulties in the way of the cosmical religion is that it leaves no room for that which religion necessarily involves, namely, love. No man will ever love anything unless he can fight for it and no man will fight for a cosmical religion. I can imagine mediæval knights with plumes flying in the air and spears glistening in the sun going out to battle in defense of their earthly Venus, but I cannot imagine astronomers with telescopes flying like plumes and measuring-rods glistening like spears, going out to battle for the astronomical Venus. I know men in whose veins flows the milk of human kindness who are willing to lay down their life for their fellow-man, but I know of no scientist who will lay down his life for the Milky Way. I know missionaries who will spend themselves and be spent for the soul of a single Bengalese, but I wonder if even Einstein will be willing to lose his finger for the spark of Betelgeuse.

It will be no answer to say that the men will lay down their lives for the Milky Way and hence will lay them down for science, for the Milky Way is not science any more than a Tom Thumb golf course or green cheese or buttermilk is science. To equate the Milky Way with science is like equating a thousand gallons of water with the Annapolis school-spirit or six hundred and forty acres of land with patriotism. The Milky Way is a thing; science is a thing related to a mind and particularly as regards its quantity and its measurement. No man would ever lay down his life for the Milky Way, for the simple reason that he will never sacrifice himself for anything that is below him in dignity and worth. A man will sacrifice himself for love of truth, but truth is something quite different from a planet. Human beings do not die for things alone but for what they believe about things. No scientist ever died for a bug. He died for the sake of humanity, which that bug was stinging. No one ever laid down his life for the stars, but some will lay down their lives for the truth that the stars bring. It is, therefore, not matter but the spirit that summons the best in man, the spirit of learning, the spirit of truth, the spirit of love—and all these are above the individual man in dignity and worth.

Being void of love, the cosmical religion must ever be unsatisfying. The human heart never can and never will love anything it cannot put its arms around, and the cosmos is too big and too bulky. That is why, I suppose, the immense God became a babe in order that we might encircle Him in our arms. And just as there is no love in the cosmical religion, neither is there truth. Truth does not mean going out to the cosmos. It means the cosmos coming into the mind. Truth is not the heavens by themselves, but rather the heavens in the head, which is the primary condition of truth. In a word, I could accept Einstein's cosmical religion if he would only leave the letter "s" out of "cosmical."

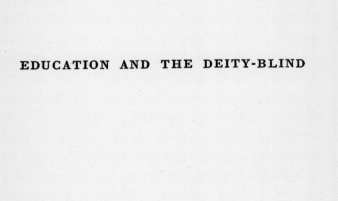

EDUCATION AND THE DEITY-BLIND

LIFE is a question of adjustment to environment. Lifeless things, such as a crystal of silica dissolved and redissolved a thousand times, will assume no other form than the hexagonal. The plant, on the contrary, possessing life, has a certain endowment of plasticity; although rooted in the soil it can adjust itself to the benediction of rain, the warmth of sunshine, and the promptings of the various seasons of the year. The animal has still greater possibilities of adjustment. It can move from sun to shade, from field to field, roam about the forest in quest of its prey, and in virtue of its sense-knowledge adjust itself to a world that is known by touch and taste, by sight, by smell, and by hearing. But when we reach man, we meet a creature who has infinite plasticity; we touch one who has a capacity for adjustment not only to work and to rest, not only to brute facts, but to causes, not only to the sciences and arts but also to Revelation, not only

267

to man but even to God. Man, in other words, has an infinite capacity for life, truth, love, and beauty; he alone of all creatures on this earth has the possibilities of attuning himself to the infinite. Since he craves the perfect and desires to be attuned to the highest, it follows that only an infinite God can satisfy him. Man above all other creatures has been made to conquer new worlds. In other words, man alone has a soul to be converted—converted to God and His holy purposes.

Education cannot be understood apart from the plastic nature of man. Taking due cognizance of it, one might say that the purpose of all education is to establish contact with the totality of our environment with a view to understanding the full meaning and purpose of life. Perhaps I can make this definition clear by an illustration drawn from astronomy. Our solar system is made up of eight, or perhaps nine, planets, with the sun as the center. This family of the sun's planets falls into two distinct groups. In the first group revolving about the sun are to be found Mercury, Venus, then our own earth, and finally Mars, each of which is smaller than our earth in size. Beyond these four minor planets extend the four major ones: Jupiter, Saturn, Uranus, and Neptune, all of which are far larger than the earth. Fourteen hundred bodies the size of the earth, for example, could be packed into Jupiter. Quite naturally these outermost planets are at an enormous distance from the sun, Neptune being more than thirty times as distant from the sun as the earth. Hence an inhabitant of Neptune, if such existed or could possibly exist, would receive only one nine-hundredth part as much light and heat from the sun as the inhabitant of the earth receives. Now let the sun represent the knowing mind, and let the eight planets revolving about the sun represent those worlds of knowledge with which the intellect of man strives to establish a contact, the conquest of which brings its own store of knowledge. Let those planets close to the sun represent those worlds of knowledge which are more visible and tangible. Without attempting to identify them in any way with my example, the four worlds revolving about the mind might be called the worlds of physical science, mechanics, astronomy, and mathematics. Out beyond these four we can imagine four other worlds of knowledge, which represent the more refined and speculative subjects, such as literature, law, art, and philosophy.

Now I repeat that the purposes of education is to establish contacts with as many knowable worlds as possible, in order to understand not only their content and their meaning, but also their purposes and their causes. Education, therefore, becomes a kind of travel to other worlds—a travel inspired by the urge of wonder that Aristotle called the inspiration of all philosophy. Like other Alexanders, once we have made any one of those planets of knowledge which are very near to us our own, we strive for new worlds to conquer, and use each conquered one as the fulcrum by which we mount to those more distant regions of refined thought where pleasures of the flesh give way to the ineffable joys of the spirit. The greater the number of worlds of knowledge conquered, the more intense becomes the pleasure of living. He who can call trees by their names, and knows the smell of the shy violet; he who can tell the speed of light, and can make a course on a trackless sea under the light of the stars, like so many glittering tapers; he who knows the history of his own people, and he who can be thrilled by a sonata of Chopin; he who can enter into contact with the world of poetry, and call the day a priest and the sun a host and see in each sunrise a host being lifted to spread benediction over the world and at night set in the flaming monstrance of the West—he, in a word, who knows not only his own world but other worlds as well, is a man who has learned not only to enjoy life but also to make this world, by virtue of his knowledge, a better place to live in.

In the definition of education it was observed that the purpose of education is to enter into contact not merely with environment but with the *totality* of environment, with an end to explaining the purpose of life. But the purpose of life cannot be understood without God, nor can any one enter into contact with the whole of environment unless he enters into relationship with God, in Whom we live and move and have our being. Imagine a man in a boat in the center of a lake. He sees approaching him a series of little ripples becoming increasingly wider and not leaving off their play until they have reached the distant shore. Now

271

the man in the boat knows that the ripples did not cause themselves. If he is to account for their existence he must look out beyond to the distant shore where perhaps stood a man who threw a stone into the lake that caused it to awake with its watery vibrations. So too, it would be necessary for any mind that sees the concentric orbs of knowledge round about him, to go out beyond the worlds to Some One who stood on the seashore of eternity and threw those planets into being from the tips of His Almighty fingers. And that Some One who explains the totality is God. No mind has entered into communion with the whole of all that is, and hence no man can call himself truly educated unless his mind has carried him out beyond the uttermost rim of space, out beyond "the margent of this world," out past "the golden gateways of the stars," out to that beauty which leaves all other beauty pain, and to that love we fall short of in all love, out to the Life of all Living—God, the Creator and Lord of the world.

The great pity of life is that so many minds fail to make an acquaintance with the whole of their environment. There are some who can enjoy the barking of a saxophone but have no appreciation for the overture of a Beethoven. There are those who discover the planet of science but have not mental telescopes strong enough to discover the world of poetry. There are others who are quite satisfied to conquer a world of business but have not power enough to conquer the world of philosophy. There are some who can enter into contact with the world of credit but fail to enter into contact with the world of faith. Such minds are content to know only a part of their environment but not the whole; they fail to adjust themselves to the whole of their environment. They are very much like the deaf who are dead to the great environment of sound: children's laughter, the voice of a friend, the song of a bird, the sweet flow of poetry, the thrill of music, the sigh of the winds, and the sadness of a waterfall. Sound and harmony constitute one of the greatest pleasures of this world, but to the deaf the world of sound is a vast and undiscovered realm. They are also like the blind who are dead to the great environment of beauty: the gesture of a friend, the flash of an eye, the earnestness of a visage, the beauty of a rainbow, the twinkle of a star, and the fall of a meteor. Beauty, too, is one of the sources of life's pleasures, but there are some who are as dead to it as if they had never been born.

Over and above the world of sounds and visible things, over and above the world even of science and philosophy, there is that still greater environment of life, truth, love, and beauty which is God, Who alone can satisfy the infinite aspirations of man. One of the sad and regrettable things in education is that there are some people in this world who are dead not only to the world of poetry, music, philosophy, but dead to the life and love of God, and that class we may call the *"Deity-blind."* This group is alive to the environment of what might be called a progressive world; its words are correct, its sense of propriety shows itself in the embellishment of homes and the choice of amusements; it is worldly; it is rich; it is sophisticated; it is successful; it is at ease; it is honored; it has eyes, but they are blind—blind to the beautiful environment of God and the Incarnate life of Christ.

The very existence of this class, even in educated circles and university life, should give us pause and make us ask questions as to whether or not we are educated, in the right and true sense of the term. It is the growing mass of Deity-blind in our American life that prompts me to submit these questions:

Are the schools and universities throughout the country that ignore God really educating the young men and women entrusted to their care? Would we say that a man was a learned mathematician if he did not know the first principles of Euclid? Would we say that a man was a skilled littérateur if he did not know the meaning of words? Would we say that a man was a profound physicist if he did not know the first principles of light, sound, and heat? Can we say that a man is truly educated who is ignorant of the first principles of life and truth and love—which is God? I submit that a little child who to-night is kneeling at the knee of a foreign-missionary sister, and learning for the first time that God made the sun, the moon, and stars that shine down upon her, and that some day she will render an account to Him as her loving Lord—that child, I say, is a more profound philosopher, a wiser scholar, a mind more entitled to university degrees, than all of our gowned professors scattered through the length and breadth of this land who know not that beyond time is the Timeless, that beyond space is the Spaceless, the infinite Lord and Master of the universe.

To leave God out of a university curriculum is to leave out the First Cause and the intelligibility of all that is, and to leave out the First Cause is to deny God; it is to inculcate a contrary prejudice. Leaving God, the source of moral obligation, out of a university curriculum is not just merely negation; it is a privation. It is not merely the absence of something, like lack of color on a wall, but it is a privation, like the plucking out of an eye. The young minds in many of our universities, by a process of refined skepticism, are not being permitted to know the beauties that lie beyond the solar system. It was just such ignorance of the whole totality of environment that explains a pathetic remark that a young student of one of our large universities made to me after having heard a sermon on the love of God: "That is not possible; if such a lovely thing had ever been, they would have told me about it." The point I am trying to make is that they have not been told, and hence the proper definition for many a modern university is "a place where five thousand students are looking for a religion and something to satisfy their hearts, and know not where to go to find it."

Would it not be well to establish universities in this country dedicated to the purpose not of learning but of unlearning? Have not the false philosophy and the false morality that certain universities have been guilty of in the last two hundred years created a distinct problem in the realm of education, namely, that of undoing what has been done badly? The time has come when a certain intellectual disinfection or sterilization has become necessary, in order that health may be restored to thinking society. Just suppose that we could endow a university in America that would unlearn the notion that drenching a mind with physics makes a man religious; suppose we had a university department that would unlearn the false pragmatic philosophy of our country, which tends to prove that all proof is worthless; suppose we had a department of religion which would unlearn the false notion that because all religions are alike in certain elements, they therefore have the same common root and foundation, and are all of human origin; suppose we had a university for unlearning the idea that progress is just mere change and complexity, instead of development in the right direction; and a school for unlearning all of the false history that has been taught under the inspiration of Gibbon. If such a university could rise within our land, wherein professors would set minds right along the lines of sanity and would root out the misconception that novelty is truth and that morality is something more than taste—that university, I say, would be doing the same service for our country that a board of health does for our city, for it would help to keep clean those mental arteries which supply the mind and the heart. If we honor those scientists who by their knowledge, industry, and effort, have held back the ravages of disease and death, why should we not honor those other men who keep back the ravages of error? For after all, if disease is possible, it may be equally true that error is possible, and the greatest of all diseases. Such a university will come into being, perhaps, as soon as we realize that our country is suffering not so much from falsehood as from the unbearable repetition of half-truths.

Is it not time to recognize that the Catholic system of education is about the only worthwhile system of education in a world that is rapidly becoming filled with school-houses? There is not a difference in degree between modern education and traditional education that we might call Catholic, but rather a difference in kind. The difference between the two is the difference between education and instruction. We educate, they instruct. Education means drawing something out, as the Latin root itself signifies. Instruction seems to mean putting something in. Now only God and the Christian order can draw something out. Man can put something in and it may either be good or bad. There can be no education in any system of training which asserts that man is just a glorified animal, or a respectable descendant of the forest, that he has no supernatural destiny, or a soul that has potentialities for communing with the infinite. Such a system, by its very nature, can never draw anything out. Our system, on the contary, asserts that we are not risen beasts but fallen angels, that we have had a Golden Age in the past when our ancestors walked with God, that we have a nature which has a capacity for being lighted with the faith of God, and becoming veritable children of the Most High God. In any theory of training, therefore, in which God is left out, character must be explained solely and uniquely by external influence, such as heredity, environment, or psychological stimuli and society. The predominance of the external is the note of barbarism. When God is asserted, character is explained not so much by external factors as by internal ones, such as self-negation, which is the highest kind of self-assertion, and an act of the will in which a man remains master of his fate and captain of his destinies.

Some students in our land are granted the blessed privilege of living under the influence and inspiration of a system of education that is not only Catholic in the religious sense of the term but catholic even in the secular sense, for "catholic" means "universal." To them has not been denied the right to know the totality of all environment and the reason of it all, which is God. When one thinks of the hundreds of thousands of young men and women who are leaving the portals of universities in this country there is reason for those properly trained to rejoice in a singular privilege: They, who have been educated in the sense in which I have defined, are the only ones of all university graduates who know why they are here and whither they are going. The least that can be expected of any college or university is that when it embarks its graduates upon the sea of life it will furnish them with a compass with which they may find their port. Students of Catholic colleges have been given this compass, which is their faith. They have been steered toward their port, which is the Kingdom of God, and they have learned that during this voyage they are carrying a precious cargo, which is the grace of God in their souls, and that even though tempest and storms do come, a day of peace will finally arrive when the moon will send down its beams like silver grappling-hooks to take them into the very bosom of God for Whom they are made. With the passing of time they will forget the refinements of Latin syntax, they will no longer remember a delicate point of the law, the year of Kant's birth or of the battle of Waterloo. Hamlet's soliloquy will fade from their memories and much of the materia medica will become a thing of the past. The one thing that will endure will be the assurance and the joy that they have reached out not only to those concentric orbs of knowledge which make the ripples of the universe, but have gone out even to the Hand that created those ripples in the immensity of space. This will be to them one of the greatest joys of life, for in the knowing that there is another world and another life, they can have a great deal of pleasure in this one. A child who is given a ball with which to play and is told that he will not receive another one, must of necessity treat that ball with a great deal of seriousness. He may not play with it too often, nor be too adventurous with it, for it is the only one that he is ever going to have. But if he is told that very soon he will be given another ball that will never wear out and which will give him more amusement than the first, he can afford to take the first one lightly, play with it as he pleases, and even

282

prick it full of pin-holes. Now those universities and colleges which have left God out of their curriculum through their inability to reason from the visible things to the invisible have told their students that this earth is the only ball they will have to play with. The result is that they have created in the minds of their students the impression that they must take the world very seriously, for they are never going to have another ball to play with. They must always live in mortal horror of their cosmic bubble's ever bursting, and hence can never enjoy it. Students trained in the whole of knowledge, which includes theology, will know that there is another ball coming later on—another life, another world. They therefore can be gay with this one, using it as a stepping-stone to God. In the light of this knowledge they can be optimists while others must be pessimists. Others must be pessimists because they say that life is too short to give a man a chance. Christian students can be optimists because they can say that life is long enough to give man a chance even for eternity.

MAKING THE STORK A BOOTLEGGER

SOUND logic is not always desirable. It is, in fact, the most dangerous of all things if one starts with a false premise. In such a case the more logically one reasons, the further one gets from the truth. The only hope there is for a healthy conclusion or a good thought, if the premise is false, is to make a terrible slip somewhere in the reasoning process. Crooked roads sometimes get us back on the right road if we have lost our way, but if the wrong road is a straight road we are lost forever.

In this connection it is worth remarking that birth-control propagandists are the most logical people in the world. Their first principle is that of the Sadducees: there is no future life. Man has within himself no spiritual principles, no purpose in this world, and no abiding victory to gain. His tent has been pitched here by cosmic floods of space-time and some day he will dissolve into the Einsteinian "field" of gravitation and electricity.

Now grant this first principle, which is untrue, apply a rigorous logic to it, and you have birth-control. If there be no purpose in being a man, there is no reason for begetting men; if there be no finality about human life, there is no use in continuing it; if there be no goal for mankind, there is no use in starting the race—not even the human race. This is perfectly sound reasoning. It is just like saying that if there is no use in one-horse shays, what is the use of making them?

Unfortunately, however, for this logic, the root principle of birth-control is unsound. It is a glorification of the means and a contempt of the end; it says that the pleasure which is a means to the procreation of children is good, but the children themselves are no good. The road that leads to Rome is good, but Rome is not; the machinery of generation is good, but the product is not. In other words, to be logical, the philosophy of birth-control would commit us to a world in which trees were always blooming but never giving fruit, a world of artists who were always picking up brushes but never finishing a picture, a world full of sign-posts that were leading nowhere.

In this cosmos every tree would be a barren fig-tree and for that reason would have upon it the curse of God.

Even though one were to admit that babies were useless, advocates of birth-control would have to admit that they would be good later on to preach birth-control. Just think what a havoc would have been wrought among the birth-control propagandists if the mothers of those who preach it had practised it! The more birth-control is practised, the less chance there is that it will ever become a permanent philosophy, for a time will come when its propagandists will have become extinct and the remnant who beget will have the world to themselves.

If this philosophy is ever to become universal, it must constantly be making exceptions and saying that in certain cases it must not be taken too seriously. Excuses or extenuations must constantly be made, and the principal one will probably be the economic one: the number of the children will depend upon the budget and the gold balance. Children must not be invited to the homes of the poor. The assumption here is that children are not wealth, an assumption that is fallacious, for children are like

289

photographs—the wealthiest friend cannot buy them. Poverty is no excuse for shutting them out any more than poverty is an excuse for a father's cutting off the head of his tenth child because he has money enough for only nine hats. It has always struck me as strange that we should pardon a wife, on the grounds of "temporary insanity," for limiting her married life by shooting her husband, and at the same time glorify the same wife as a "progressive free-born woman" because she limits her family by stifling an unborn life. All of which goes to prove that we do not need new laws but expansion of the definitions of old ones, and particularly of the law of murder.

Birth-control is the flesh-and-blood side of Prohibition—an amendment to the human constitution stating that the enthusiasm for new life must not exceed one half of one per cent. Both are equally incapable of enforcement. There is life in wine and men will have it as long as there is life; there is joy in children and men will have them as long as men love to play. As long as men feel that drinking the vintage of God's creation is not a sin, there will be bootleggers; and as long as men feel that children are the real wine of life, there will be storks— and to call the storks bootleggers will not ease the situation any more than to call the wine-peddler a bootlegger.

It is high time the thinking element of America protested against reforms based upon percentages instead of principles. It has led us into a hopeless confusion of what is right and what is wrong. Prohibition has obscured moral vision by calling a sin that which is not really a sin, with the result that a disregard for this reform-made sin has brought into the world a disregard for all that is really sinful.

Birth-control steps into this confusion and says that that which is really a sin is not a sin at all, but liberty and progress. Public consciousness absorbs this false morality and sentences a woman in one state to prison for life because she took four drinks, but lets thousands run loose who have taken four lives. Twenty-five millions of dollars is not thought too high to enforce the law of the Anti-Saloon League, but twenty-five dollars would be thought too high to enforce the law of God. Truly there is such a thing as straining at gnats and swallowing camels. The domain of morality to-day extends only to the "public" sins like drinking; the amoral is the "secret" sins, like birth-control.

The Catholic Church is said to be indifferent about the great American democracy because she does not make morals center about Prohibition; yet no one ever thinks that by opposing birth-control she alone is making it possible for democracy to survive. It is the birth-control propagandists who are undemocratic—they limit life and happiness to the aristocracy of the "sample children."

This does not mean that the restriction on spirits is on the same basis as a restriction upon children, for the latter is far more fundamental. Prohibition may be better than no liquor at all, but half a baby is no better than no baby at all. The point here is that if legislation cannot make a man decide on the percentage of his alcohol, then much less can it make him decide on the percentage of his children.

No one is quite so loud in pleading for self-expression as those who practise and preach this philosophy of birth-control. Every woman, they claim, must be freed from the chains of motherhood and the bondage of birth-giving.

But how in the name of heaven does birth-control effectively teach self-expression? Is my eye finding the best self-expression when it is blindfolded? Is my ear delighted in its individuality when it is plugged? Is my tongue finding its noblest expression when my mouth is bandaged? Why then should I say that husband and wife are finding their individuality and best expressing themselves when they stifle, frustrate, and contracept those faculties which God has given to them, and through which they may find an expression so genuine that their own individuality stands incarnate before them? The deepest wound one could have inflicted upon Michelangelo or Raphael would have been to tell either of them that a certain work of his did not measure up to the possibilities of his genius; so, too, a husband and wife who have the slightest pride in the creative artistry of their lives should deem their lives a failure if they have fallen short of what might be expected of them, and certainly nothing can be more reasonably expected of life than life.

The immorality of birth-control, then, is not a matter of authority but of common sense. It is too often said that birth-control is wrong because the Catholic Church says it is wrong. No, birth-control is wrong because reason says it is wrong; it is the misuse and abuse of certain faculties that God has given to mankind. But because the Church alone to-day upholds reason, that which reason condemns is identified with what the Church condemns, and forgetting the profound rationalism that inspires her, men babble about her autocratic authority.

Birth-control is not new, either in its enthusiasm or its methodology. Perhaps its greatest exponent was a king who was so full of it that he preached it with decrees and soldiers, and was so scientific in his method that all his "sample children" were girls; and that methodical, scientific king was Herod. The only difference between the methodology of this first birth-controller and those of our own day is that Herod's contraceptive device was a sword. And the Babe that escaped, when He grew to manhood, called the son of that king a "Fox," as if to remind him that those who practise birth-control lose manhood not only for themselves but for their posterity.

The two philosophies of life endure to our

294

own day: the philosophy of the Fox, and the philosophy of the Son. The first is known as birth-control, the second as self-expression. However much the first may protest that it is in keeping with the spirit of the age, it must forever recognize that the twentieth century is an age of productivity and a theory that throttles it is ill-becoming to our *Zeitgeist*. To answer that they hold for machine-productivity but not human productivity is to miss the point at issue, for what is the use of having machines that produce unless we also produce men to run them?

The other philosophy we have called the "philosophy of self-expression." Its transcendent beauty is grounded in the sublime truth that human begetting human is not imitating the beasts of the field but the God of the heavens. Fecundity is not a push from below, but a gift from above. Self-expression was eternal in the Godhead before it was temporal in the cosmos; generation belonged to God eternities before it was given to flesh. "He that planteth the ear shall he not hear? He that formeth the eye shall he not consider? Shall not I that make others bring forth children myself bring

forth, saith the Lord. Shall I that give generation to others myself be barren?"

From all eternity God the Father generated
a Son, the image of His substance; from that
day without beginning or end the Heavenly
Father in the ecstasy of the first and real pa-
ternity has said to His Son: "Thou art My Son,
this day have I begotten Thee." And that Divine Life eternally sealed with a perfect spiritual self-expression, came to earth as an echo of
eternity in the days of Creation; it found its
feeblest expression on earth in plants, but its
grandest in man, and from that day to this
every couple who throw down the gauntlet to
the philosophy of the Fox, who refuse to chain
their powers and throttle their faculties, who
insist on a self-expression that is another self,
are carrying on the very purposes of creation,
are imitating feebly not the animals, but God
Himself. The Heavenly Father has a Son Who
is the fulness of all the perfections of the Father, and yet from all eternity He has decreed
that other children should be born to Him and
be admitted to the glorious privilege of adop-
tive sonship in which they can say "Our
Father." This work of raising up other chil-

dren, He has committed to parents whom He has graced with a double power and privilege: first, that of shaping something in their own image and likeness as He shaped them in His own image and likeness, and secondly, that of giving to their children another "birth" in the sacrament of Baptism, in which they are "born of God," become His adopted sons, heirs of Heaven, and members of the family of the Trinity.

And as these children are destined to copy their Christian parents in the development of their natural traits, so they are expected to copy their Divine Exemplar, the Son Incarnate, Jesus Christ, in the development of their supernatural traits. In other words, children are not expected to act like beasts because they come from one, but to act like God because made in His image and likeness. Parents, in like manner, are to look upon their children not merely as children of the flesh, but as children of the spirit, for in the regenerating womb of the baptismal font they have become privileged to call God "Father," and Jesus Christ "Brother," and Mary "Mother." Perhaps the most materialistic birth-controller in the world would admit bringing a son into the world if she were certain he would become President; why should she scruple at bringing one into the world if she were certain he was to become an adopted son of God?

Such is the spiritual reason behind the family, and those who challenge it not only do not know the meaning of "Christian," but also they do not even know the meaning of "love," for love naturally tends to an incarnation, which is a birth; and incarnation naturally tends to crucifixion, which is the labor and sacrifice of birth; and the crucifixion naturally tends to the resurrection, and that is Heaven, and Heaven is a place where there are only children: "Unless you become as a little child you cannot enter the Kingdom of Heaven."

The best secrets are always hard to keep. God found it difficult to keep the secret of His own nature; He told it to man, and that was Revelation. In a more realistic way, a husband and wife who are overflowing with happiness cannot keep the secret of their joy to themselves, and the telling is the beginning of their family. God has, as it were, introduced into creation the law of decreasing monotony, the operation of which provides that a child shall break the monotony of marital dualism, and a second one break the monotony of the first, a sixth break the monotony of the fifth, and grandchildren relieve the monotony of children. But the selfish couples, who know not the joys of noble self-expression, are full of sadness and disquietude—for perhaps they have a *skeleton* in their closet.

THE MAN IN THE TREE OR THE MAN
ON THE TREE

THE MAN IN THE TREE OR THE MAN
ON THE TREE

I KNOW of at least a dozen universities in this country where a professor in all his academic seriousness has asked his students the question: "Do you believe in evolution?" To ask an intelligent man a question of that kind is like asking him if he believes in clothes. There are many kinds and styles of clothes, and there are many theories and kinds of evolution. Evolution, in general, means progress, like the unrolling of a carpet; hence, one may speak of the evolution of chicken-growing, the evolution of law, the evolution of baseball. I believe in evolution just as I believe in clothes, but as my fancy in clothes does not run to Scottish kilts, nor to wooden shoes, nor to the uniforms of deep-sea divers, so neither does my intellectual fancy run to the antiquated materialistic evolution of the type of Haeckel's, or to the idealistic evolution of the type of Hegel's. Evolution is the constant, and its particular theory and scope is the variant, just as clothes are the constant, and swimming-suits are a variant. Hence, to confuse Darwinism with evolution is like confusing balloon-trousers with pants. A man may be an evolutionist without being Darwinian, just as a man may be civilized without wearing lace sleevelets. There are, it must be remembered, about 57 varieties of evolution, most of which are more or less acceptable working hypotheses in the empirical order. Evolution is a much bigger problem than the one that asks which came first, the monkey or the organ-grinder. The sane outlook on evolution may be summed up in some such propositions as the following.

1. Evolution does not exclude God. Evolution means growth or progress, and therefore clashes with no theology or philosophy, and involves no fundamental issue. Evolution is in answer to the question *how* things take place; God is the answer to the question *why* things take place. I may say, for example, that this watch was made by machine, or that it was made by hand. The machine-process would imply that the watch was made by one operation and at one time; the hand-process would

304

imply that it was made gradually and over a long period of time. In either case, I would be explaining *how* the watch was made; but when that question was answered, there would still be room for the more fundamental one: "Who made the watch?" So too with the universe. Evolution maintains that the plant and the animal gradually evolved one from the other. But this still leaves as an open question: "*Who* made the things that evolve?" Evolution, in other words, no more excludes God than the fact that a man is self-made excludes his mother.

2. The length of time required for the universe to evolve does not dispense with the necessity of a Creator. There are some minds who live under the impression that if one dwells on the millions and millions of years it took for the universe to unfold itself, one does away with the necessity of accounting for a cause. But God could do things slowly as well as quickly, simply because He is outside time. To say that length of time dispenses with a cause is just like saying that if the handle of a brush were long enough it would paint by itself, or if the legs of trousers were sufficiently long they would never have needed a tailor to cut them.

The tortoise demands a progenitor as well as the hare who won the race. The problem, then, is not whether things are going fast or slow, but *why* they go at all.

3. The smallness of the original "stuff" or gas or matter from which the world might have evolved does not dispense with the necessity of a First Cause. Just as there are some who believe that a *long time* makes God unnecessary, so there are those who believe that a *tiny speck*, from which the universe gradually unfolded, renders Him unnecessary. The existence of God, however, is not based on the bulk of the universe, but on the fact that it does not account for its own existence. Even though the speck from which this universe came was no larger in volume than a pin-point, God would be necessary to account for (1) the reason of its being as a static thing; (2) the motion with which it was endowed as a dynamic thing, and which motion permitted it to unfold its latent energies; (3) a plan according to which it would evolve, for unless there was a purpose for evolution, there would be no reason why the primordial speck should ever start to evolve.

But it is often asserted that while the original speck could not account for its own existence, the sum of its various products added together would account for it without an appeal to God. But this is a vain subterfuge, for one would be merely adding together insufficient things, and just as a thousand idiots never make a wise man, so neither could a thousand worlds that transmitted energy be the final source of that energy. The canal would be prolonged, it is true, but the lengthening of a canal never makes a source. One is therefore driven back to a First Cause. But it may be asked: Who made the First Cause?

Such a question does not understand what a first cause means. First Cause means first not in the order of *time*, but in the order of *reason*; it means self-sufficiency, and to ask that the First Cause be in its turn caused, is to ask that a First Cause be at one and the same time and under the same formal consideration a secondary cause, which is a contradiction.

4. Not even the theoretical question of the eternity of the universe dismisses the necessity of a First Cause. It is not by *reason* but by *revelation* that we know the world had a beginning

in time. Reason of itself, St. Thomas Aquinas teaches, could never prove that the world began. But there are other sources of knowledge than reason, and the source that is faith has assured us that the universe did have a temporal beginning. Hence the question of the eternity of the world is a "theoretical" one.

The time-problem or the beginning of things must not be confused with the ontological problem or the reason of things. Even though the world were eternal, it would still be eternally dependent upon God. I can imagine an eternal seashore on which there is an eternal footprint. But the footprint must have been made there from all eternity. Eternity in time is quite another question from eternal dependence.

5. The supposed conflicts between faith and science concerning evolution are due to a false notion of what constitutes the rule of faith. Almost all discussion on the presumed conflict between science and religion assumes the Protestant position to be the true one. The Bible, according to the Protestant theory, is the rule of faith, and therefore is fundamental in deciding religious questions. According to the

Catholic doctrine the Bible is not fundamental, for a man's first principle cannot be the Bible, but what he *believes* about the Bible, namely, that it comes from God. The Bible is not a book, but a collection of books, and hence more like an anthology. One therefore cannot start with it any more than one could with an encyclopedia. The fundamental problem, then, is not what the Book says, but who gathered the books together; who decided that it would begin where it does, and leave off where it does; who decided that certain books presumably written by contemporaries of Christ would not be included, and other books written later on would be included. When one answers these questions one has gone beyond the Book to an organization or a Church that, as the continued life of Christ on earth, decided that the Bible was inspired, and which from that day on has decided the meaning of its passages, just as in another way the Supreme Court of the United States decides the meaning of difficult passages in the Constitution of the United States.

When therefore certain agnostics and skeptics, bent on discrediting religion, allege that there is a contradiction between the "seven days" of Genesis and the known facts of science concerning the great age of the earth, they are really attacking the Protestant conception of the Bible as "fundamental," but not the Catholic theory that something preceded the Bible. Individual interpretations of Fundamentalists have emphasized the necessity of adhering to the seven days of Genesis as seven days of twenty-four hours. Not so with the Catholic Church and its Supreme Court of interpretation. In 1909 the Biblical Commission stated that in the denomination and distinction of the six days mentioned in the first chapter of Genesis, the word *"yom"* (day) can be taken to mean either in its proper sense a natural day of twenty-four hours, or in an improper sense any indefinite period of time.

The whole position of the Church in this matter has been summed up by one of its great scholars, Knabenbauer, in these words: "Considered in connection with the entire account of creation, the words of Genesis proximately maintained nothing else than that the earth with all that it contains and bears, together with the plant and animal kingdoms, has not produced itself nor is the work of chance, but

310

owes its existence to the power of God. However, in what particular manner the plant and animal kingdoms received their existence: whether all species were simultaneously created, or only a few which were destined to give life to others: whether only one fruitful seed was placed on mother earth, which under the influence of natural causes developed into the first plants, and another infused into the waters gave birth to the first animals—*all this the Book of Genesis leaves to our investigations and the revelations of science, if indeed science is able to give a final and unquestionable decision.* In other words, the article of faith contained in Genesis remains firm and intact even if one explains the manner in which the different species originated according to the principle of the theory of evolution."

It is time, then, that those who speak of the supposed conflict of religion and science make a distinction between kinds of religion as they make a distinction between kinds of science. The rule of faith of Protestantism is not the rule of faith of Catholicism. The Catholic Church does not make the Bible a book of science, nor does she as a Church concern herself with secondary causes; these she leaves to the domain of science, whose province it is to gather facts and formulate hypotheses and laws, which are to be verified and controlled by other facts. The Church has never made an official interpretation of the Book of Genesis as to the age of the universe, or as to the length of time it has been unfolding; she has said nothing concerning the origin of life on earth or even on the possibility of life coming from matter. Despite this fact, there are some who maintain that if it could be proved by science that life came from matter, the whole structure of Christianity would collapse. It perhaps might interest those who hold such a false position to know that many of the Scholastics believed in spontaneous generation, and if such a thing were ever proved we would once more be back to the days of the wise Scholastics.

6. The Church has defined nothing concerning the possible origin of the body of man from a lower organism. Here again the same distinction must be made between the so-called "Fundamentalist" position, and the Catholic position that goes beyond Fundamentalism, which is very clear. First, the Church has de-

fined nothing concerning the immediate origin of man's body within the meaning of the words of Sacred Scripture: "From the slime of the earth." Secondly, if to-morrow it could be proved that the body of man were evolved from a lower animal, it would not be found to contradict any official teaching of the Church. Thirdly, the attitude of the Church toward the evolution of man's body might be described as prudently scientific: the view that man's body evolved from a lower animal is at the present time an unproved hypothesis, and hence the Church believes it would be unwise and imprudent to reject the old traditional view that the body of man was created immediately by God, in favor of the new and uncertain, even though such a view would not be contrary to her decisions.

Now certainly this sane, calm, balanced outlook should commend itself even to those not of the faith, and they should admit that her point is very well taken, for two reasons: because of the nature of the facts themselves, and because of their weight and quantity. In dealing with such a thing as the possible animal origin of man, one must go by evidence and not by experiment. Evidence is never as convincing as experiment. There is no such thing as experimenting with a fossil bone to see if it would become a human body, in the same way in which one might experiment with a battery to see if it would throw a spark. The mistakes of experiments can be corrected, but inferences about evidence cannot. There is great danger of going astray in the field and of wrong ideas going to one's head like that wine on an empty stomach, and therefore extreme caution is necessary. Furthermore, the Church's attitude of prudence is borne out by the quantity of the facts themselves. There is an impression abroad to the effect that the facts of the animal origin of man's body are overwhelming. Such, however, is far from the truth. An unprejudiced authority, Mr. Gerrit S. Miller, Jr., of the Smithsonian Institution, Washington, makes these two remarkable statements: "As a result of seventy years of effort, these tireless workers [in search of fossils] have made exactly two 'finds'—no more." And hence in his opinion "we should not hesitate to confess that in place of demonstrable links between man and other fossils, we now possess nothing more

314

than some fossils so fragmentary that they are susceptible of being interpreted either as such links or as something else."

In conclusion, then, the hypothesis that man's body evolved from a lower organism is not opposed to the teaching of the Church, but it is only a hypothesis. And hence because the missing link between man and the animal has not been found, the Church still prefers with science to call it the "missing link."

7. Though it is not intrinsically impossible that the body of man might have evolved from a lower organism, it is absolutely impossible that the soul of man could have so evolved. It must be remembered that the belief in the soul is not founded on the grounds of faith alone, but also on reason. I believe in a soul not only because faith tells me there is a soul, but because my two intellectual lobes functioning properly tell me there must be one. Faith comes to the aid of my reason, confirms its conclusions on this point, and makes my reason for believing in a soul ironclad—and even fool-proof. In another chapter the existence of the soul was proved by the fact of laughter; here another argument is presented, drawn principally from the existence

315

of art, to show that the soul of man could not have evolved from the beast.

Art is the expression of the ideal through the real. To do the same things over and over again through necessity, like beavers building dams and birds their nests, is not art, though it may be instinct. In order that man produce art, he must have ideals, ideals which he expresses through the medium of matter. He must have, for example, such ideas as "justice" or "truth," "bravery" or "honesty." But no one has ever been out for an automobile ride with "Justice"; no one has ever sat down to a meal with that ideal called "Truth"; no one knows the latitude or longitude of "Bravery." These ideals are spiritual. Where do they come from? One cannot get blood out of a turnip, nor can one get grapes from thistles, nor figs from thorns, nor can we get thoughts, which are not material, from matter. These ideal thoughts, since they are spiritual, must have been produced by a principle capable of producing spiritual things, and that we call a soul. Art, then, which is the expression of the ideal through the real, is not the result of an evolution but is a new emergent in the universe—

316

something that emerges with the appearance of a soul in man.

The early birds who got the early worms did not fashion their nests after the Greek temples, nor did the later birds build their nests according to Norman lines of architecture, nor do our present-day birds gather up the forked twigs to express the piercing piety of Gothic. Canaries have never idealized their great songsters by erecting monuments to their great operatic stars, nor have sea-gulls ever idealized their heroes of long flights by erecting tablets to their Lindberghs. The caterpillar was not an Impressionist and the butterfly not a Post-impressionist. The zebra was not a Cubist and the leopard a Futurist. The solemn and inescapable fact is that one never meets art in the true sense of the term until one meets man. The earliest records we have of man, namely, the cave-man, are records proving that he was not an animal and also proving that he was an artist, and the records are writings and paintings on walls.

"We should not have to dig very deep to find a man drawing a picture of a monkey, but we have never dug deep enough, nor will we ever dig deep enough, to find the records of a monkey drawing the picture of a man. There may be a long lost trail of broken bones concerning the origin of the body of man but there is nothing even faintly suggesting the development of a mind." [1]

Art, in other words, is the signature of man. He is not only a creature but a creator, a creator by virtue of the spiritual power within himself that can produce ideal forms, which ideal forms can be translated into matter—and that spiritual power is the soul.

In conclusion, then, man is not an evolution but a revolution. He may be an animal but he also has a soul. He is the only animal in the world that is not a domestic animal. Every other animal in this world seems to belong to this world and is content with it. Man is the only wild animal in the sense that he is not domestic in his longings and aspirations; because of his soul, he has an infinite reach toward the infinite life, love, and truth of the God Who made him.

8. Neither sound faith nor right reason discountenances a search for the missing link. I

---

[1] G. K. Chesterton: "Everlasting Man."

think we should seek for the link—not the link
that will bind us to the beast, but the link that
will bind us to God. I can't see that our family
tree looks the more beautiful because there is
an animal hanging in it. Why glory in the link
that binds us to the beast? Rather let us seek
the bond that binds us to God. And where is
that bond? In a cave most certainly, but not in
the cave of Java—in the cave of Bethlehem.
And the name of the one in that cave is not
"Cro-Magnon" but "Christ,'" and the animals
in the cave are not jointed animals, but the ox
and the ass at the Master's crib. The light shining in His eyes is not the light of a beast coming to the dawn of reason, but the light of God
coming to the darkness of man. The compan-
ions of the Babe are not ape-men but shepherds and kings, and the woman in the cave is
not a monster but a Virgin Queen.

There are then only two possible theories
concerning the nature and dignity of man: one
is that life is a push from below, and the other
that it is a gift from above. According to the
first, man is supposed to act like a beast because
he came from one; according to the second, he
is expected to act like God because made in His

own image and likeness. The source of our dignity is not to be sought by looking for a *man in a tree* but rather by looking to the *Man on the Tree*. The man in the tree is the beast swinging from his tail in the selfish joy of his bestiality. The Man on the Tree is Christ Jesus in the ecstatic beatification of His redemption. The man in the tree is the beast-man. The Man on the Tree is the God-man. The man in the tree looks forward to a progeny of the children of animals, and the Man on the Tree looks forward to a progeny of the children of God. The man in the tree looks back to the earth whence he sprang. The Man on the Tree looks upwards to the heavens whence he descended. To the man in the tree, all the other trees of the forest bear only the burden of leaves. To the Man on the Tree, all the other trees of the forest bear the burden of penitent thieves. When the man in the tree dies, not even the leaves chant a requiem. When the Man on the Tree dies, even the earth yawns and gives up its dead, for it is the Tree that matters now as in the beginning when man balanced a fruit against a garden: *Et qui in ligno vincebat in ligno quoque vinceretur.*

PETER OR PAN

THE story of the development of new paganism is the story of the Prodigal Son. The younger son in the parable is Western civilization, who in the sixteenth century goes to the spiritual father of Christendom and asks for a share of the substance garnered through the centuries. The spiritual father gives Western civilization a share of that capital in the shape of the necessity of a Church, the Divinity of Christ, the inspiration of Sacred Scriptures, the existence of God, and the necessity of religion. In the course of the last four centuries, Western civilization has been prodigal of that patrimony. In the sixteenth century, it spent its belief in the Church, in the seventeenth, the inspiration of Sacred Scripture, in the eighteenth, the Divinity of Christ, in the nineteenth, the existence of God, and in the twentieth, the necessity of religion. At the present day, the capital is all gone and now it is feeding on husks, under the names of "New Thought" and "Progress." It was not

323

so long ago that the father of Christendom could depend upon those sects that called themselves Christian to help defend the great fundamental truths of Christianity, such as the Divinity of Christ and the necessity of the salvation of the individual soul. That day is past. Many of the best-known preachers are to-day teaching nothing but a glorified Humanism and there are but few who would dare to speak of divine justice or retribution. We are, therefore, practically forced to carry on the battle for Christian truth alone, and this is something new in the history of Christianity.

In our day the religion of Christ is facing a crisis such as it has not faced, probably, since the days of Constantine. By that I mean that up to this time the Church has been engaged in a kind of civil war, in which a Christian idea has battled with a misunderstanding of a Christian idea or in which sect has fought with sect. None of the great heresies of the first sixteen hundred years of the Christian era denied the existence of God, but they had misconceived the notion of the Trinity, the nature of Christ, the nature of Divine Grace, and the mission of the Church. In the last four centuries the conflict

324

was not so much of idea and idea as the conflict of sect and sect. To-day we are faced with something entirely novel. We are engaged now not so much in what might be called a civil war, but we are confronted with what Mr. Belloc has called "an invasion," that is, a force of ideas that is as strange to traditional Christianity as Christianity was strange to Paganism. This new invading force is New Paganism. New Paganism may be defined as an outlook on life that holds to the sufficiency of human science without faith, and the sufficiency of human power without grace. In other words, its two tenets are: Scientism, which is a deification of the experimental method, and Humanism, which is a glorification of a man who makes God to his own image and likeness.

New Paganism is not the same as the old Paganism. The most important differences between the two are these: the old Paganism was a confusion. New Paganism is a divorce. The old Paganism did not deny God, in fact it asserted supreme powers, such as Zeus and Jupiter and the "Unknown God of Athens." What it did, however, was to confuse divinity and humanity, matter and spirit, God and man, to such an extent as to reduce them to a kind of unity. Thus it was that idols of gold and silver, of marble and brass, were called "gods." There was much that was reprehensible in this kind of theology, but there was also something that was noble. Why did the pagans make their gods in sensible forms like statues? Merely because in their ignorance they could make no distinction whatever between spirit and matter? May it not be more likely that in making their gods visible in matter, they were dimly expressing an instinctive yearning in the human heart for an Incarnation, or a God amongst men? May it not be that Bethlehem was the realization of those crudely expressed pagan ideals? And the very fact that idolatry passed out of the world with the knowledge of the Incarnation proves in some way that the human heart has had its cravings satisfied and its ideals realized.

New Paganism, on the contrary, does not confuse the human and the divine—it separates them, it divorces them. It runs a sharp sword of cleavage between the things that God joined together and forbade to be put asunder, that is, such tremendous realities as God and the cosmos, nature and grace, faith and science, body and soul, morality and conscience, husband and wife, maternity and Providence, divine action and human liberty. After having divorced the two, New Paganism immediately throws away the better half and lives worse with the other half. That is why to-day there is religion without God, Christianity without Christ, and psychology without a soul. That is why there are Behaviorism, Humanism, and all the other new labels. From this point of view, the old Paganism was preferable to the new, for at least it acknowledged the necessity of some power above man, even though it was only a household god who by his wrath might put down the fever and fervor of birth-control.

The second difference between the old and the new Paganism is that the old Paganism worshiped the vital forces of nature and entered into vital communion with them and the cosmos by some sort of ritualistic magic that belongs to the domain of religion. New Paganism continues to worship the forces of nature, but it enters into communion with this cosmic order not by a ritualistic magic that belongs to the realm of religion, but by a mathematical formalism that belongs to the domain of science. The old Paganism with its ritualistic magic had the advantage of admitting the worshiper into some dim borderland of the unknown and providing him with an inspiration and awe that is foreign to the New Paganism, with its clockwork cosmos of pointer-readings and shadowy configurations of space-time. The old Paganism found a God, though it was only an unknown God. New Paganism finds a God—and its name is Man.

The third difference resides in the nature of the two kinds of paganism. The old Paganism was the perversion of *natural* lights and misuse of reason by those who could have come to a knowledge of the invisible God from the visible things of the world. This was the basis of St. Paul's reproach to the Romans. New Paganism, on the contrary, is a perversion of *supernatural* lights, the putting out of the flame of Christianity and the light of faith and the revelation of Christ Jesus. The old Paganism put out the light of the candle of reason; New Paganism put out the light of the sun of Faith. The only way to understand the degradation to which man had fallen is to know the heights from

328

which he had fallen, and no one will deny that it is impossible to fall from a greater height than the hope and life that Christ brought to this world, and in this sense the fall of New Paganism is the greater.

What will be the future of New Paganism? If present religious and philosophical conditions continue, it is not unlikely that the religious universe within the next century or two will be divided into two great worlds—the world of Peter and the world of Pan. First of all, that group in our society which believes in the existence of God, the Divinity of Christ, the necessity of redemption and spiritual sanctification, those who put on the panoply of Rome though they have not yet her soul, those who are outside of the Church but honestly seeking and praying for truth and light, will, by the very logic of their ways, slowly, surely, certainly, and inevitably end in the veneration of Peter or the Church of Rome. That other group, on the contrary, which babbles and prattles about the omnipotence of science, which believes that the idea of God must be suited to the new astrophysics and that a future life is a survival idea from uncivilized peoples—this

329

group, I say, will by the very logic of their ways, slowly, surely, certainly, and inevitably end in the worship of Pan or Paganism. But there will be no more Peter Pans, no more Federations of Churches, no more "broad-mindedness." We shall be either hot or cold. We shall either gather with Christ or we shall scatter. The day of compromise and time-serving will have passed.

And then what will be the issue? There probably will come a conflict of these two forces. For just as no nation can exist half slave and half free, so, too, Christianity cannot exist half Christian and half pagan. If the present indications mean anything, the conflict of Peter and Pan in some future day will be translated into the conflict between the forces that worship the State and the forces that worship God. As men cease to believe in God, the State becomes God. The great and tragic scene before Pilate will be reënacted, in which the Church as Christ must always be misunderstood by the world, and in that future day as in the days of the old Paganism, another Tertullian will arise to plead for justice as the first Tertullian pleaded in the year 193:

330

"As to the Emperor and the charge of high treason against us, Cæsar's safety lies not in hands soldered on. We invoke the true God for the Emperor. Even if he persecute us, we are bidden pray for them that persecute us, as you can read it in our books which are not hidden, which you often get hold of. We pray for him because the Empire stands between us and the the end of the world. We count the Cæsars to be God's vice-gerents and swear by their safety (not by their genius, as required). As for loyalty, Cæsar really is more ours than yours; for it was our God who set him up. It is for his own good that we refuse to call the Emperor god; Father of his Country is a better title. No Christian has ever made a plot against a Cæsar; the famous conspirators and assassins were heathen, one and all. Piety, religion, faith are our best offering of loyalty."

As the world becomes better in one direction it will become worse in another. As it becomes violent in one direction, it will become saintly in another. As the individual hates his body, restrains it, mortifies it, persecutes it, his soul grows better, more spiritual, more refined, more saintly. Such is the meaning of the words

331

of our blessed Lord, "If you wish to save your life, you must lose it." What is true of the individual is true of the race. As it becomes wicked, it will also become saintly. As Pan becomes powerful, so Peter will become powerful. As the Church is persecuted and seems to be on the very threshold of death, it will be spiritually alive, awaiting its resurrection, as Christ was, even when He was laid in His tomb.

This intensification of the forces of good and evil can have only one issue and that issue will be—persecution and apostasy. Apostasy, because shallow minds will be affected by the New Pagan doctrine of the sufficiency of human knowledge without faith; persecution, because shallow hearts will be affected by the New Pagan doctrine of the sufficiency of human power without grace. Apostasy will be pride in action or the temporary supremacy of the fads and fashions of the age over the unchanging truths of eternity. Persecution will be Humanism in action or sentimentality gone mad. Persecution is a form of social sadism in which society takes pleasure, as perverted individuals do, in the infliction of pain. It comes

332

not only with cold-bloodedness but also with hot-bloodedness, which is degeneration.

Christ has never promised his people earthly peace and repose, but He has promised them persecution. "As they have hated me, so will they hate you." Every nation or group of people that has become particularly dear to Christ, because prosperous in the affairs of the soul, has become so through persecution. England paid for her faith by blood and that blood is now the purchase price of her reconversion. France paid for her title as the eldest daughter of the Church in the Western world by the blood of the French Revolution. Ireland has paid for her faith so many times over as to be one of the peoples in the world whom God loves most. We have twenty million Catholics in this country who have not been bought with blood. Will they have to pay the price for that faith? Will they have to suffer to rise to new heights? Will they escape the law that Good Friday is the prelude to an Easter Sunday?

If persecution comes, when will it come? No one knows but God. But one thing is worth observing so far as the future is concerned.

There are appearing in our periodicals at the present time a series of articles many of which have for their avowed purpose the destruction of everything Christian, God-like, and Christ-like. These articles, some of which have been critically appreciated in these pages, still belong to the realm of theory. But how long can they be kept in the world of theory? How long does it take an idea to work itself out of two covers of a text-book into the great broad world? How long will it take the atheistic doctrines of many of our universities to ooze their way out through the four corners of a class-room and become translated into the language of the man on the street? How long will it take man to seize upon these ideas not as theories, but as principles of living? Fifty years ago, Darwin's theory was a class-room theory. Now most people are living under the illusion that they have read Darwin, and many talk evolution as if they knew whereof they spoke. Even already everybody is talking about Einstein, though few know what Einstein is talking about. It may take longer for the immoral theories of self-expression ethics and the godless philosophy of space-time to work themselves into the very marrow and fiber of the common man. But when these ideas do work themselves out, then we shall have persecution or perhaps Sovietism. The only difference between the theory of godlessness of the Soviet State and the temper and tone of the articles I have mentioned, is the difference between theory and fact. Sovietism does not write its articles in the learned journals but writes its beliefs with blood on church steps. It does not write against sanctuaries; it abolishes them. Sovietism is not concerned with the thrill that comes from "a bold challenge to morality," but with the animal satisfaction that comes from the burning of a flame of hate in the very sancturary lamp of God. It is Pan in action.

If that condition of godlessness is ever to be averted, if Paganism is ever to be thrust back, it can be met with only one force in the world, and that is the Church—and by that word, I mean the Church, not churches. The Church is the only thing in the world that knows anything about Paganism. She was born not of Paganism but in Paganism. She saw it grow; she saw its gods dethroned; she saw its State worshiped. But she also saw it decline, and we know, and all history knows, that the only reason Paganism declined was because of the civilizing and supernaturalizing power of Christ in His Church. The Church assisted at the death-bed of Paganism. The last beast of Paganism was fed on the body of one of her faithful. The last god that was overthrown was cast to earth by a convert to Christ from Paganism. Now, as then, the Church is the only force that knows it, and when the modern world calls it new, we remember it as something old. As the modern world looks upon it as something progressive, we look upon it as the degradation of barbarism. We know that if it must be crushed again, as it was crushed of old, by a surrender of our lives and our blood, we are willing to do it. When that conflict will come, if it comes, we know not; we know nothing of its details, nothing of the alignment of forces; we know not the kind of swords that will be unsheathed—but there is one thing that we do know, and that is that in that struggle with the powers of darkness and the errors of Paganism, in that warfare of Peter and Pan, if Truth wins, we win. If Truth— Ah! But Truth can't lose!